A Grower's Guide to

Herbs

Text by Geoffrey Burnie & John Fenton-Smith
Photographs by Lorna Rose

CRESCENT BOOKS
NEW YORK

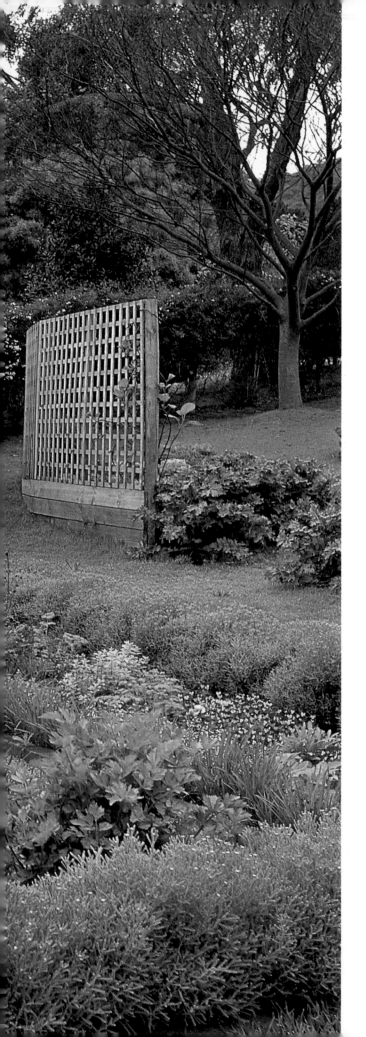

CONTENTS

LEFT: A formal herb garden need not be very large or elaborate. Here a simple cross pattern of brick paths is centered on a lead statue and framed in cotton lavender.

ABOVE: The pretty leaves of salad burnet.

GROWING HERBS

No garden is complete without a few herbs, which are mainly used to add flavor and delight to food, but which have many other uses, too: in cosmetics, craft arrangements, herbal remedies and as good companions and edging plants in the garden. They can usually be purchased, of course, but you will feel extra pride when using herbs you have grown yourself. And herbs are almost all very easy to grow.

To a botanist a herb is a plant that does not have a permanent woody stem: that is, one that is not a tree or shrub. Its edibility is irrelevant. Gardeners have a different definition. To them, a herb is a plant that can be added to food or used for medicinal purposes, even if the plant in question is actually a shrub, such as rosemary, or even a tree, such as the bay tree. Herbs are (or may be) used fresh, unlike spices, which are almost always dried or prepared in some other way first. (Spices, such as pepper or nutmeg, are the seeds, flowers, bark or roots of tropical trees or shrubs.)

LEFT: A pink and gray border of pinks, lavender and thyme harmonizes in this herb garden with old-fashioned roses, although they are not yet in bloom.

THE RICH GREEN COLOR and the soft texture of parsley makes as elegant a garnish for flowers as it does for a dinner plate. In this stunning garden it is used as contrast with miniature blue violas and white sweet alyssum.

USING HERBS

Today we use herbs most often when preparing food. Any cook knows how useful it is to have some herbs on hand. Even a pinch of dried herbs from the supermarket can make a great difference to a so-so dish, but the same herbs fresh from the garden can add the savor and scent that makes the dish something special. Restraint, however, should be the order of the day. The recipe will be your guide, but remember that dried herbs are often sharper in flavor than fresh ones and fresh herbs vary in strength with the season. Add a little at a time, tasting as you go: you don't want to taste the herb before you taste the food. Go easy, too, in planning the menu. One herbed item on the plate is usually sufficient.

Herbs are used extensively in flower arrangements and crafts, where they add fragrance and different textures. Herbal potpourris and wall hangings are especially effective and herbs can be used in home-made cosmetics for those who want an alternative to commercial preparations.

Herbs are also credited with all sorts of medicinal qualities. In the past it was an essential part of a doctor's education to learn to distinguish beneficial herbs from useless and harmful ones, and these studies laid the foundation of the modern science of botany. Some of the old prescriptions have been verified by science and many modern drugs are still extracted from plants, although other old remedies were apparently based on nothing more than wishful thinking and superstition. (Sometimes the patient may have been merely suffering from a shortage of vitamins which a salad of green herbs made good.) The folklore attached to herbs is part of their charm, but don't dabble in herbal cures without seeking advice from your doctor or a reputable herbalist first.

HARVESTING HERBS

The traditional way to gather herbs is to pick them just as they are coming into flower (when the flavor is strongest) and use them immediately. This way you use them at their best and most attractive.

Many herbs can also be used after they have been dried. You can spread them out on a table to dry in the shade for a couple of days or, these days, the microwave oven provides a more than acceptable alternative. Gather the herbs, spread them on a paper towel, cover them with another paper towel, and zap them with the full power of the microwave for a minute or two. Check them, and if they aren't quite dry, give them some more time with the top towel off. The precise timing depends on what sort of herb it is and how dry the leaves were to start with.

Alternatively, you can freeze the fresh herbs. Just roll them up in plastic wrap, pop them in the freezer and take what you want when you need them.

CHOOSING HERBS TO GROW

Whether you plan to plant an extensive collection of herbs or just a few, your first choice will obviously be the ones you like best, those that feature in your favorite recipes or craft activities. (Chances are you'll probably already have them, dried, in your kitchen.) It is probably a good idea to grow several plants of these herbs to avoid harvesting them to death. However, don't let unfamiliarity stop you from trying out a plant or two of a herb with looks or fragrance that appeal to you.

PLANTING HERBS

It is a time-honored tradition to grow herbs in gardens of their own, and if you have the enthusiasm and the space, a small formal herb garden with its beds divided by paths arranged around a central feature such as a statue or a sundial can be very pretty. Most herbs are low growing, and few are all that distinguished in appearance—indeed, some are rather weedy-looking. Marshaling them into formal beds flatters them, and you can play their subtle foliage colors and textures off against one another. You might, for instance, contrast the gray leaves of sage with the lush green ones of parsley, or the featheriness of dill with the rounded solidity of rosemary; and the variegated and fancy-leaved versions of such herbs as sage, balm or mint will enrich your palette.

If a formal garden is not for you, don't despair. There will be a place for herbs in any garden, for they really are very adaptable. Try one of the following ideas.

• Plant herbs in your flower beds. Being mostly low growing, they are best planted at the front, where their subtle greens and grays will set off the bright flowers behind.

• Plant them along the edges of your paths, where they will release their scent on the air as you brush past.

• They can look especially well in front of roses—and they will hide the rose bushes' thorny legs—but be careful if you have to spray the roses. You won't want the spray drifting onto the herbs and rendering them dangerous to eat.

• Be strictly utilitarian and plant them to edge the beds in the vegetable garden. Here they will give you something to look at when the beds are bare between crops.

• Most varieties grow very well in pots, which means that even if all the garden you have is an apartment balcony you can still have the pleasure of fresh herbs.

• Give your herbs a windowbox on the kitchen windowsill so that you can just reach out and harvest as you need them— but only if the window gets the sun, and make sure they are outside in the fresh air. Magazines are full of pictures of pots of herbs growing in the kitchen itself, but herbs are not indoor plants. They survive inside for a few weeks, but they get straggly and leggy and you won't get much of a harvest.

• However you choose to deploy herbs in your garden, don't plant them too far from the kitchen door. Nothing is more frustrating than to find you need a sprig or two for some dish and have to make an expedition to the bottom of the garden while a pot boils over.

PROPAGATION

Most herbs can be grown from seed, but it can be a slow process and most gardeners start with purchased seedlings or by taking cuttings or dividing plants. The appropriate method for each plant is discussed under its entry.

MAINTENANCE

Growing herbs is easy. As a general rule, they love sunshine and don't need much watering: indeed the flavor is richest if they aren't encouraged to grow too lush. They don't, however, appreciate being starved so give them good, well-drained soil and some fertilizer occasionally. The main exceptions to the rule are basil and chives, which do best with generous feeding and regular watering, and bergamot and the various mints, which are lovers of damp soil. Most herbs have few specific pest or disease problems. You'll find more detail about requirements and problems in the description of each species.

ROOTING A CUTTING

If you are going to root a herb from a cutting, take the cutting from a strong, healthy plant early in the morning. The cutting should be 2–4 in long. If you are not able to plant it at once, wrap it in damp newspaper and keep it in a cool place.

Remove the lower leaves and prepare a small pot with a mix of two-thirds coarse sand and one-third peat moss. Make a hole with your finger or a pencil where the cutting is to go, insert the cutting to about one-third of its length and firm the mix around it. Water well and then cover the pot with a plastic bag to create a mini-greenhouse effect.

Keep the mix damp but not wet. Once roots have formed, the plant can be planted out in the garden.

1. TO TAKE A STEM CUTTING, cut just below a leaf (node or joint). Do not bruise the stem, and trim the end of the cutting with a razor blade if need be. Prepare a pot, making sure it has adequate drainage so excess water drains away.

2. INSERT ALL THE CUTTINGS into a pot (or several pots), first making a hole in the soil with your finger for each cutting and then firming the earth gently around the cuttings. Space the cuttings around the edge of the pot.

3. THEN WATER THE CUTTINGS in well but gently, taking care not to dislodge them. Make sure the container has adequate drainage holes so that the excess water will drain away. If the soil remains too wet, the cuttings will rot.

4. MAKE A WIRE OR BAMBOO FRAME that fits around the pot and is tall enough to clear the cuttings. Place a plastic bag over the frame and pot: the bag will keep the air and soil moist. Place the pot out of the direct sun.

ALOE VERA

Aloe barbadensis, syn. *A. vera*

FEATURES

A bitter-juiced, succulent perennial, aloe vera grows to about 7 ft high and wide in the open garden but is much smaller in containers where growth is restricted. A strong, fibrous rooting system supports a single, sturdy stem that can be up to 3 ft tall and shows many leaf scars. The fleshy, pale green leaves, which can grow to 2 ft long, are lanceolate with spiny, toothed edges. The pendent, bell-shaped flowers are yellowish to purple and are borne on long branches (racemes) in summer, while the capsule-like fruits are triangular and contain numerous seeds.

CONDITIONS

Climate Best grown in tropical and warm zones.
Aspect Prefers full sunlight and good drainage. The leaves may turn brown in harsh sunlight, and so the plant is often grown indoors in direct light, but growth will be slow if the light is too poor. Protect from heavy frosts or the plant will freeze.
Soil Grows in almost any soil as long as it is reasonably open and water drains rapidly—the roots will rot if exposed to long periods of wet soil. If soil and water are too alkaline, growth may be slow.

GROWING METHOD

Planting Can be grown from seed but more often by division of the parent plant. New shoots must be "pruned" or leaves will turn bright green and grow horizontally rather than vertically. When new shoots are 4 in tall, break them off from the parent and repot in soil made up from equal parts of coarse river sand, garden loam and decayed garden compost or cow manure. Water well, then leave for 3 weeks to form a network of water-seeking roots.
Watering Do not overwater; in the wild it is used to alternate wet and dry periods. Allow the plant to become fairly dry in between watering and water only very lightly during winter. Water more often during the growing period when the leaves and stem begin to thicken.

LIKE MOST SUCCULENTS, aloe vera grows very well as a pot plant on a sunny windowsill. Its pale flowers are not very exciting.

Fertilizing Excessive fertilizing may slow growth.
Problems Problems are almost non-existent, but watch out for root rot in wet soils.
Pruning The plant grows from the center, and so older, outside leaves need to be cut to keep the plant in balance and in shape. These leaves do not grow back once cut.

HARVESTING

Picking Harvest leaves as required but always cut larger, lower leaves first as they have more juice. This also promotes new growth from the center. Trim the thorny edges of the leaves and split the leaf across its width to extract the gooey gel. As the gel ceases to flow, scratch the exposed leaf and continue to do so until only the green leaf skin is left.
Storage Whole or partially used leaves can be wrapped in foil and stored in the refrigerator for several days, or the extracted juice can be bottled.
Freezing Can be frozen for 6 months.

USES

Cosmetic The juice of the leaves is applied directly to the skin as a softening agent and for minor wounds (insect bites, scratches or cuts) and sunburn. Astringent and drying, it is often combined with lanolin and vitamins A and E to intensify its soothing qualities.

ANGELICA
Angelica archangelica

FEATURES

Growing up to 7 ft tall with a spread of around 5 ft, angelica is a majestic, stout-stemmed, perennial herb with big, toothed leaves made up of several leaflets. The tiny, honey-scented, greenish yellow flowers are produced in clusters in spring; winged seeds follow later in the summer. All parts of angelica are subtly, sweetly aromatic.

CONDITIONS

Climate Only really suited to cool climates as the plant needs to rest over winter. In frost-free areas it is soon exhausted by continuous growth.

Aspect In cold climates where summers are mild, grow in full sun. Where summers are hot, part shade is essential. Shelter from wind.

Soil Needs well-drained but moisture retentive and fertile soil. In the wild, angelica often grows in damp woodlands or by streams.

GROWING METHOD

Planting Can be grown from seed sown as soon as it is ripe. Sprinkle seeds onto a tray of moist seed-raising mix and barely cover. Keep evenly moist. Expect germination in 3–4 weeks but germination is not always reliable. For a few plants, lift two-year-old plants in early spring and divide roots into smaller sections. Replant immediately into loose, friable fertile soil.

Watering Keep soil moist and pay particular attention to watering in summer. The plant is native to cool, rainy areas and does not tolerate dryness.

Fertilizing Apply complete plant food once in early spring when new growth begins and again in early summer. Mulch around plants with compost or rotted manure to feed and condition the soil.

Problems Angelica is short lived, usually dying after two years, but if it doesn't flower it grows for up to four years: snip off flower stems as they form.

Pruning No pruning is necessary. In cold climates it dies back to the ground each winter.

ACCORDING TO LEGEND, the healing properties of angelica were revealed to a medieval hermit by the angel Raphael—hence the name.

HARVESTING

Picking Collect the seeds by harvesting the whole flower head just as it ripens. Place in a paper bag in a warm, dry place until the seeds fall from the head. Separate the seeds from the dross before storing. For best flavor, cut stems after bloom but leaves may be picked at any time. Roots are dug just as flowers are forming and washed clean immediately.

Storage Store seeds in an airtight jar. Crystallize stems before storage; leaves are dried and ground before being stored in airtight containers. Clean roots can be stored in a cool, dry, dark and airy place until needed.

Freezing No parts of the plant are suitable for freezing.

USES

Culinary Crystallized stems and leaves are used as sweets and to decorate cakes. Leaves can also be used to make a herbal tea.

Medicinal Tea made from any part of the plant can be taken to soothe nervous conditions and to ward off colds. Frequent or heavy consumption of any part of the angelica plant should be avoided as it is known to exacerbate certain medical conditions. Diabetics should avoid the plant altogether.

Craft Use dried stems, leaves and roots in potpourri.

Gardening Angelica is a handsome plant that makes an attractive addition to a planting of perennial flowers in cool climates.

ANISE
Pimpinella anisum

FEATURES

A dainty, feathery-looking annual that may reach a height of 2 ft, anise has rounded, green leaves with distinctly toothed edges. The flat heads of white flowers appear during late spring or summer and are then followed by the small, licorice flavored seeds—aniseeds.

CONDITIONS

Climate   A summer annual, anise can be grown in all areas.

Aspect   Full sun is essential but the site must be sheltered from strong winds which will flatten this light, airy herb.

Soil   Light, sandy, well-drained soil enriched with rotted organic matter is ideal for this plant but anise grows well enough in any friable, well-drained soil.

GROWING METHOD

Planting   When spring has definitely turned warm, sow seeds where they are to grow about ½ in deep and 6 in apart. For its seeds to ripen properly, anise requires a long, hot summer and in cooler areas where summers may be short or mild it is advisable to start seedlings early. Sow them indoors in late winter or early spring into trays of seed-raising mix. Place in a sunny window on a heated seed-raising pad and keep lightly moist. When seedlings are big enough to handle, prick out into small individual pots and place these on the heated pad. Plant out only when the weather has turned warm.

Watering   Anise needs moisture around its roots at all times and must never be allowed to dry out. To avoid flattening the stems, water the soil rather than the leaves.

Fertilizing   Grown in average well-drained garden soil and mulched with rotted manure or compost, anise will not need further feeding. If soil is friable but poor, dig in a ration of complete plant food at planting time and mulch when the seedlings are 8 in tall.

Problems   No particular problems.

THE ROMANS flavored wedding cakes with anise, thus starting (it is sometimes said) the tradition of rich cakes at wedding banquets.

HARVESTING

Picking   When the flowers have finished the seeds will begin to grow and ripen. When fully ripe, remove the seed heads and place them on paper or in a container in the sun to dry out. Don't allow dew to settle on them overnight or expose them to rain. Fresh leaves can be picked as they are needed.

Storage   When the seed heads are fully dry, rub the seeds to separate them from the husks and store them in airtight jars.

Freezing   Not suitable for freezing.

USES

Culinary   Seeds give a pleasant, licorice taste to many types of cooked foods including cakes and pies, stewed fruits and vegetable dishes. The seeds are also said to be an aid to digestion. Fresh leaves may be used in salads or added late to casseroles, stews and soups.

Medicinal   This is a good tonic for the digestive system and regular intake of aniseed is said to help prevent colds and to banish bad breath. Taken before bed, aniseed encourages sound sleep.

Craft   Aniseed is used in making potpourris and pomanders.

Gardening   Anise is strongly attractive to bees and butterflies and will bring them to the garden.

APOTHECARY'S ROSE

Rosa gallica var. *officinalis*

FEATURES

A prickly shrub that can reach a height of 5 ft, apothecary's rose is a dense bush that spreads by suckers, often forming impenetrable thickets. The fragrant, semi-double, crimson flowers appear in late spring and are followed in autumn by dull red hips. Leaves are elliptical in shape and leathery.

CONDITIONS

Climate From southeast Europe and western Asia, apothecary's rose is best suited to cool climates but grows satisfactorily in warm and arid areas.

Aspect Full sun is essential and in warm climates an open site with good air movement helps reduce the ill-effects of high humidity. Shelter from drying summer winds in hot, arid areas.

Soil Grows in a wide range of soil types but drainage must be good, especially in areas of high summer rainfall. Deep, friable clay-loam with plenty of rotted organic matter is best.

GROWING METHOD

Planting Can be grown from seed collected from ripe hips in autumn but sown in spring, or from suckers detached from the parent plant in late winter. Each sucker must have its own roots; replant at once. Take hardwood cuttings about 8 in long in late autumn; insert them into potting mix or vacant garden beds and keep moist. Roots form over winter and can be potted up or planted into the garden in spring.

Watering Established plants can survive on rain alone in areas of regular rainfall but the plant will look and flower better if it is given an occasional deep soaking during dry times and in summer.

Fertilizing In good, fertile soil, one application of complete plant food in early spring is enough. Mulch with rotted organic matter to improve the soil, feed the plant and conserve moisture.

Problems Suffers from the usual rose problems: aphids, caterpillars, scale insects and fungus diseases, especially in humid areas. Combined insecticide/fungicide, usually sold as "rose spray," controls aphids, caterpillars and fungus diseases. For scale insects, spray affected stems with dormant oil in winter.

THE "RED ROSES" in old recipes always meant the apothecary's rose, but you can substitute any sweetly scented red rose from your garden.

Pruning Does not need annual pruning and can be left alone for years. To rejuvenate an old bush, cut stems to the ground in winter.

HARVESTING

Picking Ripe hips are harvested in autumn when fully ripe; flowers can be picked for immediate use as they appear.

Storage Both hips and flowers may be stored for a few days in sealed containers in the refrigerator.

Freezing Rose hips and flowers are best used fresh.

USES

Culinary Rosehips are made into jellies, syrups and liqueurs (all have a very high proportion of vitamin C). Petals are used to flavor vinegar or are crystallized and eaten as a sweet.

Medicinal Infusions made from the hips and/or petals are said to be good for headaches and a range of other common complaints such as diarrhea, fever, mouth ulcers and toothache.

Craft Hips and petals are used in crafts. Dried petals are added to potpourris. Attar of roses, an essence extracted from the flowers, is a perfuming agent.

Gardening This makes a good large-scale groundcover, barrier planting or hedge. Highly perfumed, vivid flowers appear once a year.

BASIL

Ocimum basilicum, O. sanctum

SOME COOKS think purple-leaved basil 'Dark Opal' is less sweetly flavored than the ordinary green one; others detect no difference.

THE FLOWERS of the common green basil are not very exciting, and some people prefer to pinch them off to promote more luxuriant foliage.

PLANT BASIL where you sit in summer and you won't be bothered with flies or mosquitoes. This is the "cinnamon-scented" variety.

FEATURES

Most basils, including sweet or common basil (*O. basilicum*), are annuals, but perennial varieties are also grown. They include lemon basil (*O. basilicum* 'Citriodorum'), bush basil (*O. basilicum* 'Minimum') and sacred or holy basil (*O. sanctum*). All basils have an over-riding and specific aroma and taste, depending on the variety. Their colors range from yellow-green to dark green and purple, and the small, white flowers that appear in summer produce tiny, dark brown seeds. Basils grow into bushy plants, between 12 and 32 in tall, and usually have silky-leaved stems. The ruffle-leaf and lettuce-leaf varieties have crinkly leaves. Most basils make ideal pot plants, and annual forms such as dark opal (*O. basilicum* 'Purpurescens') make manageable small plants.

CONDITIONS

Climate — Grows best in warm to hot climates as it is very sensitive to cold and frost. In cold areas grow it indoors in containers.

Aspect — Prefers full sun to partial shade. Needs protection from winds and some shade in tropical areas.

Soil — Needs rich, moist, well-drained soils that are not too acid. Add plenty of compost, animal manures and lime or dolomite when preparing beds. Mulch soil during very hot or dry weather, but not until the soil has warmed up as basil roots need heat for growth.

GROWING METHOD

Planting — Plant seed in late spring to early summer in warm zones, and in summer when the soil has warmed in colder areas. Sow seeds directly into the garden to a depth of 1 in, covering them with a light seed-raising mix. Firm down and moisten the soil. Germination is usually quick, within 3–5 days. Thin out seedlings to 8 in apart. Seeds may also be germinated in seed trays using a moist mixture of vermiculite and perlite or a good quality seed-raising mix. Soil temperature needs to be warm, between 77 and 86°F. Cover the tray with clear plastic to hasten the process. Transfer seedlings to 2 in pots after a week and then transplant into open beds from mid-spring onwards.

IF YOU LOVE FRESH BASIL in cooking, you need to grow plenty of it. Planting an assortment of the different types, as in this elegant herb garden, gives interest to the eye, and you can choose which you prefer for a particular dish. They can also be combined for a wonderful blend of flavors.

Watering   Water regularly as basil likes moisture.

Fertilizing   Feed occasionally with a nitrogen-rich liquid fertilizer, especially if the plants are growing in containers.

Problems   Some beetles and slugs feed on leaves and stems causing extensive damage to the foliage. Remove the insects by hand or set shallow beer traps in damp soil among the plants.

Pruning   Keep the centers pinched to inhibit flowering and promote a bushier plant.

HARVESTING

Picking   Fresh leaves can be picked at any time or harvested and dried during late summer. Whole sprigs may also be cut after flower buds have formed but before they open.

Storage   Leaves and sprigs may be preserved in oils or vinegars. Leaves can also be dried and stored in airtight jars. Bunches can be placed in water and kept for a few days in the refrigerator.

Freezing   Wrap the sprigs in plastic wrap. They can be frozen for up to 6 months.

USES

Culinary   Basil is a very popular culinary herb, especially in Italian, Mediterranean and Thai cuisines. Leaves and flowers are used in salads or as an aromatic garnish. The leaves are also used in combination with other herbs in tomato, vegetable and meat dishes. Leaves and sprigs may be preserved in oils, vinegars or butters, where they add their own particular lemon, cinnamon or varietal flavor.

Medicinal   Basil tea is a useful remedy for travel sickness.

Craft   Basil is much prized for its fragrance and is used in potpourris and sachets. The flowering stems are sometimes used in small bouquets and other floral arrangements such as wreaths.

Gardening   Basil is a popular companion plant with organic gardeners, who believe that planting it next to tomatoes and peppers will improve their growth.

BAY TREE
Laurus nobilis

FEATURES

An aromatic, evergreen tree 20–65 ft high, the bay is often grown in containers where the height can be controlled. The trunk has smooth, gray bark and the short stalks bear alternate, shiny, dark green, elliptical-shaped leaves with wavy edges. The leaves are 1–2 in long and leathery in texture and are the edible part of the plant. The inconspicuous yellowish-green flowers, which appear in spring, produce dark purple or black, one-seeded berries.

CONDITIONS

Climate   Best grown in a Mediterranean-style climate with hot, dry summers and cool, wet winters.

Aspect   Prefers full sun in cool to warm zones but needs partial shade on very hot summer days if growing in tropical areas.

Soil   Needs moderately rich and well-drained soil. If the tree is in a container, add lime if the soil is very acid, ensure that the pot is large enough for the root ball and add decayed animal manure or compost if necessary. Mulching the top soil is always beneficial.

GROWING METHOD

Planting   Not often grown successfully from seed; fresh, green shoots or tip cuttings taken in autumn and summer offer the best chance of success. Take a 3 in cutting from a mature plant and remove the upper and lower leaves. Dip the end in hormonal rooting powder to speed up root growth. Place the cutting in a small pot containing a mix of two-thirds coarse sand and one-third peat moss. Place the pot under a plastic bag, making a wire frame to hold the bag off the cutting. This mini-greenhouse provides a warm, humid environment. Cuttings may take 9 months to take root, before they can be planted in the garden.

Watering   Bays tolerate dry conditions: let the soil dry out between waterings. However, during hot weather keep the moisture up, and pay special attention to specimens in containers.

Fertilizing   Apply complete plant food once in spring, and then mulch with rotted organic matter. Keep mulch away from the trunk.

LEAVES OF THE BAY TREE crowned the brows of ancient heroes, and it is an old belief that no harm can come to a house where it grows.

Problems   Scale, a small wingless insect covered with a waxy substance, may suck the sap of the plant and cause stunted growth. Secretions attract ants, promoting sooty mold. Treat with insecticidal soap sprays.

Pruning   Pruning is only necessary if you want to restrict the height or formalize the shape.

HARVESTING

Picking   Leaves may be picked early in the day throughout the year and then used fresh or dried as required.

Storage   Dry in a dark, airy room. Place leaves on a firm, flat surface and weigh them down to prevent curling. Leave for at least two weeks. Store dried leaves in sealed jars.

Freezing   Wrap the leaves in plastic wrap; freeze for up to 6 months.

USES

Culinary   Excellent as a flavoring in soups, stews, sauces and custards. Bay is also used when cooking game, in terrines and in pickling brines. Bay leaves are an essential component of the bouquet garni.

Gardening   This very slow-growing tree casts dense shade. It is sometimes pruned into formal shapes when grown in containers.

BERGAMOT
Monarda didyma

FEATURES

A member of the mint family with a pungent citrus-like flavor, bergamot can reach 3 ft in height. There are annual, biennial and perennial varieties with brilliant scarlet red, purple, pink or white flowers in summer. Bergamot is semi-dormant during winter, sending up squarish stems in spring and bearing dark green, ovate leaves with toothed margins. The colorful flowers attract bees and this herb is therefore a good companion for plants that need insect pollination. Bergamot is also known as bee balm.

CONDITIONS

Climate Best in cool climates and low humidity.
Aspect Prefers full sun; tolerates partial shade in fertile, humus-rich soils that hold moisture.
Soil Grow in a humus-rich soil containing a lot of organic matter such as compost and animal manures. Mulch well with leaves, straw or compost to retain moisture and keep down weeds around this shallow rooting herb.

GROWING METHOD

Planting Grow from seed or by root division, but seeds are very fine and often unreliable—this herb is easily cross-pollinated and plants may not be true to the parent in color or form. Plant seeds during spring in trays of seed-raising mix, covering the tray with glass. Seeds germinate within 2 weeks. Transplant seedlings to the garden when they are 3 in high. More reliable is root division in spring: take sections of runners or sucker shoots from the outside of the clump, which will have roots throughout the bed. Discard the center of the clump and pot the other sections. Plant out in the garden when they are growing strongly, with a distance of 32 in between each clump.
Watering Water well—like all mints, bergamot requires lots of moisture at all times.
Fertilizing Apply complete plant food at planting time and dig in. Give another application of fertilizer each spring.
Problems Powdery mildew is a white mold on the upper surfaces of leaves that causes the foliage to wilt and brown. Rust gives a reddish tinge or black waxy pustules to foliage. Remove diseased plants immediately from the garden.

MOST COLORFUL OF HERBS, bergamot is indigenous to the Americas. Native Americans brewed Oswego tea from its leaves.

Pruning In late autumn prune the plant back close to ground level. It will regenerate in spring. To increase the strength of the plant, cut flower heads before they bloom in the first year.

HARVESTING

Picking As soon as leaves turn yellow, cut the plant to within 1 in of the soil surface as this may promote a second flowering in autumn. Leaves for making tea are stripped from stems both just before and just after flowering. The colorful flower petals can also be harvested.
Storage Leaves can be part dried in a shady place for 2 or 3 days and then drying can be completed in a very low oven. Flowers do not store well and so should only be picked as required.
Freezing Wrap sprigs in plastic wrap. They can be frozen for up to 6 months.

USES

Culinary Fresh leaves can be used in summer fruit drinks or punches, and fresh flower petals are good for decorating salads. Leaves are also used for making tea.
Craft Dried leaves can be used in potpourris.

BETONY
Stachys officinalis

A BREW OF BETONY LEAVES was greatly prized by the Romans as a cure for hangovers, but perhaps our wine is different from theirs, for it doesn't seem to be as effective today. It still seems to provide some relief for headaches, though.

FEATURES

Betony is a spreading perennial with many erect stems growing up to 3 ft in height but often less. It has hairy, rough-textured, gray-green leaves that are biggest around the base of the plant. Spikes of purplish, pink or white flowers appear on long, lavender-like stems during late spring and summer.

CONDITIONS

Climate   Originally from Europe and western Asia, betony prefers a cool climate but grows successfully in warm areas. It is not suited to tropical heat or to humidity.

Aspect   Full sun and an airy, open position are best.

Soil   Any average well-drained garden soil will suit this plant.

GROWING METHOD

Planting   New plants are most easily established by lifting and dividing a big, mature plant in mid-autumn or, in cold areas, early spring. Replant the divisions, each with its own roots, immediately. Cuttings are another way to start new plants. Take 3 in long cuttings of new growth in late spring. Establish them in containers of moist, sandy potting mix and plant them out when about 8 in tall.

Watering   Betony will always look and grow best in gardens where the soil is kept evenly moist.

Fertilizing   If grown in fertile soil, a ration of complete plant food applied once when new growth begins is all that is needed.

Problems   No particular problems.

Pruning   Pinch out tips of new growth in spring to create a more compact, bushy plant. Cut stems to the ground in late autumn.

HARVESTING

Picking   Pick stems, leaves and flowers in summer.

Storage   Tie cut stems together and hang them upside down in a dark, airy place to dry. Break and crumble the dried parts into airtight jars.

Freezing   Not suitable for freezing.

USES

Medicinal   Tea made from the dried stems, leaves and flowers is taken to relieve headaches and other minor pains. It is said to be a general tonic.

Gardening   Today, betony is grown mostly for its looks. It is an attractive addition to mixed flower borders or can be used informally or to edge paths or formal plantings.

BORAGE

Borago officinalis

FEATURES

A fast-growing annual or biennial growing to 3 ft tall, borage bears star-shaped flowers with protruding black anthers in summer. They are usually bright sky-blue, although they can sometimes be pink or white. The bush bears many sprawling, leafy branches with hollow stems, which can be quite fragile. The stems are covered with stiff white hairs and the grayish-green leaves are also hairy.

CONDITIONS

Climate	Grows in all climates except extreme cold.
Aspect	Prefers sunny locations but grows in most positions, including partial shade; needs plenty of space. Borage grows quite well indoors if the pot is placed in a sunny corner.
Soil	Grows well in most soils that are aerated, moist and mulched to keep competitive weeds down. Indoors, borage needs a deep pot, and the potting mix must be moist and more fertile than is necessary for garden soil.
Support	The brittle stems may need staking to prevent wind damage.

GROWING METHOD

Planting	Sow seed directly into the garden in clumps and thin out the seedlings later, leaving 3 ft between plants. Seedlings do not transplant well once established. Successive sowings of seeds every 3–4 weeks after winter frosts have disappeared will extend the harvesting period. The plant self-sows readily and its spread may need to be controlled. Propagation by tip cuttings is also possible. Take cuttings from a mature plant in spring and pot them up, using a coarse sandy mix. Dampen the soil and cover the pot with a plastic bag supported on sticks or a wire frame. When cuttings have taken hold, plant them out in spring or summer.
Watering	Keep the soil moist at all times; during spells of hot, dry weather borage plants should be kept well watered.
Fertilizing	Apply complete plant food once each spring or use controlled release granules.
Problems	Borage is generally free of specific pest and disease problems.

IN THIS GARDEN blue borage and white garlic grow side by side. In the old days, soldiers ate the flowers of borage to give them courage

HARVESTING

Picking	Pick the leaves as required while they are fresh and young. Harvest the open flowers during the summer months.
Storage	The leaves must be used fresh—they cannot be dried and stored. The flowers can be crystallized and then stored in airtight jars.
Freezing	The leaves cannot be frozen. The flowers may be frozen in ice cubes.

USES

Culinary	Borage has a faintly cucumberish taste and leaves can be added to salads. Flowers may be frozen in ice cubes for cold drinks, or used to decorate cakes and desserts if crystallized. Note it may be a danger to health: it is now under study because of the presence of alkaloids.
Gardening	Borage is regarded as an excellent companion plant in the garden, especially when it is planted near strawberries.

CARAWAY
Carum carvi

FEATURES

Light and airy, caraway is a biennial plant growing to around 2 ft in height on slim, faintly striped stems. Leaves are aromatic, finely cut and ferny, and in summer the plant produces heads of small, white flowers. These are followed by ridged, dark brown seeds. The edible, carrot-like roots are white.

CONDITIONS

Climate   Equally suited to cool or warm climates, caraway can be successful in rainy tropical areas if grown in winter.

Aspect   Full sun is best but caraway will tolerate a few hours of afternoon shade. In windy areas, shelter is desirable.

Soil   Deeply dug, good quality, well-drained soil gives the best results and allows the roots to grow straight and long. Soil that contains rotted organic matter is the most fertile.

GROWING METHOD

Planting   Grow from seed sown in early spring or, where winters are not cold, in autumn, directly where the plants are to grow. Sow the seeds shallowly, 6–8 in apart, or thin to that spacing after germination. Mulch around the plants with compost, rotted manure or salt hay to condition the soil and conserve the moisture in the soil.

Watering   Caraway has no special water needs but will not do well if it is allowed to dry out for long periods. Water deeply during dry times.

Fertilizing   Dig a ration of complete plant food into the soil before planting and water plants with liquid organic or soluble fertilizer once or twice during late spring and summer.

Problems   No particular pest or disease problems but to prevent an invasion of caraway seedlings, remove the seed heads before the seeds fall.

HARVESTING

Picking   Seed heads are picked when thoroughly ripe but before the seeds have begun to fall. To thoroughly dry them, place them in open containers in the sun. Leaves are edible too, but the young, spring leaves are the most palatable. Pick as needed. Roots are also best used when young and small and the whole plant should be pulled up in late spring.

CLOSELY RELATED TO CUMIN, caraway has a milder, sweeter flavor but it can be used as a substitute for cumin in many recipes.

Storage   Store dry seeds in airtight jars after separating them from the dried seed head. Roots may be stored in the refrigerator for a few weeks. Leaves are eaten fresh.

Freezing   Caraway is not suitable for freezing.

USES

Culinary   Seeds are used in baking and added to many other recipes, especially vegetable and fruit dishes and curries. They can also be used to make a herbal tea. Leaves may be added to salads, and roots can be steamed or boiled and eaten as a vegetable.

Medicinal   All parts of caraway are good for the digestion and kidneys, and the seeds are often chewed after heavy meals to relieve gas and bloating.

Gardening   Sowing a succession of caraway plants in heavy, not very friable soil improves its tilth.

CATMINT

Nepeta x faassenii, N. cataria

FEATURES

There are several varieties of catmint or catnip, all with slightly different growing habits, but in general this is a low-growing perennial reaching between 12 and 36 in high. Fine white hairs cover both the stem, which is square as in all members of the mint family, and the gray-green leaves. These are coarse-toothed and ovate, although the base leaves are heart-shaped. The tubular summer flowers are massed in spikes or whorls. White, pale pink or purplish blue in color, they produce very fine seeds. Cats find some species of catmint very attractive.

CONDITIONS

Climate   Like other members of the mint family, catmint can be grown in most climates but it is not well suited to lowland tropical regions. In arid regions it needs to be given a regular supply of water.

Aspect   Prefers full sun to partial shade. The fragrance is stronger in good sunlight.

Soil   Most well-drained soils are suitable for catmint but it does best in light, organically enriched sandy loams. Dig in lime or dolomite if the soil is too acid.

GROWING METHOD

Planting   Catmint self-sows readily by seeding, once it is established, and can also be grown from cuttings taken during the spring months. To do this, cut a 4 in piece from the parent plant, remove the tip and lower leaves, and place the cutting in a thoroughly moist soil medium. Cuttings take root in 1–2 weeks. They are very sturdy and can be planted out into the garden. Water in thoroughly. Mature plants can also be divided into three or four clumps in early spring.

Watering   As members of the mint family have a high water requirement, keep this plant moist at all times. Do not stand pots in water, however, as this can drown the plant.

Fertilizing   Feed with nitrogen-rich fertilizer such as poultry manure in spring for more leaf growth.

Problems   Catmint is basically pest free.

Pruning   Prune back each year to keep bushes in shape.

THE POWDER BLUE FLOWERS and softly aromatic leaves of Nepeta x faassenii *are most attractive to human eyes and noses.*

HARVESTING

Picking   Pick fresh leaves as required. Cut leafy stems in late summer when the plant is in bloom. Hang them to dry in a cool, shady place.

Storage   Strip leaves from dried stems and store in airtight jars.

Freezing   Leaves can be wrapped in plastic wrap and frozen for up to 6 months.

USES

Culinary   Fresh young leaves were once a popular salad ingredient and were used for herbal teas, although they are less popular now.

Craft   Dried flowers and leaves are used in potpourri mixtures, and in cat toys.

CELERY
Apium graveolens

FEATURES

This popular vegetable grows to 10 in tall with erect, succulent, semi-circular stems and bright green, aromatic leaves. If it is not cropped, the plant will produce flowers and then seeds. All parts of the plant are edible, and they can be used in a wide range of herbal remedies.

CONDITIONS

Climate   Can be grown from tropical to cool climates but does best in cooler areas.

Aspect   Full sun is essential.

Soil   As celery should be grown fast, plant into well-dug, very fertile soil. Digging in well-rotted manure will improve the soil fertility and condition.

GROWING METHOD

Planting   In all areas sow seeds in spring. In warm and tropical regions they may also be sown through the summer. Sow seeds ¼ in deep into trays of fine seed-raising mix. Water with a fine mist spray and keep evenly moist. Seedlings can take up to three weeks to emerge and when about 1 in tall should be gently pricked out and potted into small, individual containers of quality potting mix. Grow on in these for around two months, and then plant out into a prepared bed.

Watering   Keep plants evenly moist always and remember that the plants have shallow roots. If they are allowed to dry out, the stems become bitter and stringy.

Fertilizing   Ensure that the bed in which celery is planted contains plenty of rotted organic matter and feed the plants biweekly, both in their pots and when they are in the ground, with liquid or soluble fertilizer that contains a high proportion of nitrogen.

Problems   Snails, slugs, aphids and caterpillars all find celery attractive. Inspect plants frequently for signs of damage—pests can often be picked off by hand. If chemical control becomes necessary, use a product with the lowest toxicity available (pyrethrum, garlic or fatty acid based sprays are examples).

AFTER THE HARVEST, allow celery plants to flower and you can gather the ripe seeds to flavor soups and casseroles.

HARVESTING

Picking   Outside stems can be picked individually or the whole plant can be harvested when mature. Small quantities of leaves can be picked at any time but the leaves perform a vital function for the plant and must not be continually stripped. If seeds are wanted let a few plants go to seed; the stems may be too stringy to eat.

Storage   Seeds can be stored in airtight containers. Leaves can be dried and similarly stored. Stems are best used fresh, but they can be frozen. Cleaned roots can be stored in the crisper bin of the refrigerator for a month or more.

Freezing   Stems cut into sections and blanched in boiling water can be frozen for several months.

USES

Culinary   Use stems in salads, soups and stews; dried leaves can be crumbled and used as flavoring.

Medicinal   Seeds, chewed whole or made into tea, are a diuretic and help eliminate toxins that aggravate gout and arthritis. Stems and leaf stems share this action and are more palatable. A tincture made from celery root has a history of use as a remedy for kidney and arthritic disorders. Juice, made from the whole plant, is said to be good for bladder infections.

CHAMOMILE

Chamaemelum nobile, syn. *Anthemis nobilis*

CHAMOMILE FLOWERS are pretty but the foliage is attractive in itself. When used as a lawn, plants will tolerate a little wear.

CHAMOMILE GROWS HERE between stepping stones to make an informal path. It gives off fragrance as you walk on it.

FEATURES

This perennial herb is known as Roman chamomile and should not to be confused with the erect and much taller growing annual form known as German chamomile (*Matricaria recutita*). Both forms have feathery foliage and flower from late spring to late summer. The daisy-like blossoms are white with a yellow center, and have many uses, ranging from use in a herbal tea to companion planting. Chamomile lawns can add interest to the garden. Chamomile has an attractive apple-like fragrance and flavor.

CONDITIONS

Climate   Grows in most climates, from hot to cool.
Aspect   Prefers full sun, but grows well in areas with partial shade.
Soil   Prefers a lime-rich soil; add lime if necessary.

GROWING METHOD

Planting   Plant seeds in spring in well-fertilized garden beds, or they may be raised in trays of seed-raising mix and then pricked out into 3 in pots to establish before being planted out. Dig and rake the area before transplanting the seedlings during spring. For a lawn, prepare the area over winter. The seed can then be spread or sown directly into a prepared lawn bed. Finely rake the bed to cover the seed and water it in. Keep the lawn weeded. Alternatively, rooted cuttings or offshoots of the parent plant may be taken and set out in well-manured soil, 18 in apart. In cold areas they will need heavy mulching to survive severe frosts.

Watering   Keep soil evenly moist; do not let it dry out.
Fertilizing   Give light applications of bone meal during spring and autumn.
Problems   No specific pests or diseases worry this herb.
Pruning   Chamomile lawns can be mowed and will regenerate quickly.

HARVESTING

Picking   Pick flowers as they appear during late spring and summer, just as the petals start to turn backwards from the central yellow disk.
Storage   Dry flowers on paper on racks in a cool, airy space, and then store them in airtight jars.
Freezing   Flowers can be frozen for up to 6 months.

USES

Cosmetic   Chamomile flowers are used to make face masks and hair rinses.
Culinary   Popular as a herbal tea.
Craft   Flowers are used in potpourris.
Gardening   As a companion plant, chamomile keeps a range of other plants happy and healthy, especially cucumber, onions and other herbs.

CHERVIL
Anthriscus cerefolium

FEATURES

Chervil is a small, hardy annual herb that has a long cropping period. Looking rather like parsley, it grows to about 12 in, the small, light green leaves turning pinkish in hot, sunny weather. Only the lower leaves have stalks. The leaves are usually curly but there is a variety with plain ones. Very small, white flowers are borne in clusters (called compound umbels) during the summer. The herb has a very subtle flavor, somewhere between anise and parsley.

CONDITIONS

Climate   Grows best in a cool climate but tolerates humid tropical areas.

Aspect   Prefers filtered shade during summer and survives over winter if kept in the sun. Ideal for growing indoors in a sunny position.

Soil   Needs to be rich in compost and well drained. Add lime to strongly acid soils. Mulch plants against extremes of temperature.

GROWING METHOD

Planting   Successive plantings every 2 weeks until the weather becomes too hot ensures a long harvest period. In the garden, plant under or near larger plants that provide shade and protection. Chervil does not transplant well, and so sow seeds into their final position. Cover only lightly, even exposing the seeds to the sun a little, but keep the seeds moist. Germination is within 10 days. Thin seedlings to 10 in apart when they are 2 in high.

Watering   Water well as moisture is essential at all times.

Fertilizing   Side dress occasionally with a soluble and nitrogen-rich fertilizer to promote leaf growth.

Problems   No specific diseases but aphids can be a pest. Treat with appropriate sprays as vigorous hosing does not seem to work.

HARVESTING

Picking   Chervil leaves are ready to cut from about 6–8 weeks after planting.

Storage   The leaves can be made into a herb butter. The leaves are not really suitable for drying: they can be dried rapidly in an oven but they do tend to lose their flavor when undergoing this heating.

THE PRETTY LEAVES of chervil lose their parsley-like flavor when cooked. Sprinkle them over dishes just before serving.

Freezing   Herb butters can be wrapped in plastic wrap and stored in the freezer.

USES

Culinary   Both stems and leaves can be used as a flavoring in foods. Fresh whole sprigs are used in salads or they can also be used to make an attractive garnish. If you are using chervil in cooking, be sure to add it at the end of the cooking process, because long periods of heating will result in it gaining a bitter flavor. Chervil is one of the main ingredients of *fines herbes* used in French cooking. It can also be used effectively in herb butters.

CHICORY
Cichorium intybus

FEATURES

This large perennial plant sometimes reaches over 3 ft in height. It has intense sky-blue, fine-petaled flowers, borne in summer, that open in the morning but close up in the hot midday sun. The broad, oblong leaves with ragged edges, reminiscent of dandelions, form a rosette around the bottom of the tall, straggly stems. The upper leaves are much smaller, giving a bare look to the top of the plant. Chicory is an attractive background plant but it sometimes needs support to remain upright. If cultivated by forced growth and blanching, the lettuce-like heart of the chicory plant is turned into the vegetable witlof, or Belgian endive.

CONDITIONS

Climate Suitable for most climates but not usually long lived in the tropical areas.
Aspect Prefers full sun.
Soil These plants require deep, rich, friable soil for best growth. Dig in plenty of organic matter in the form of compost or decayed animal manures before planting. Keep the garden beds free of weeds.

GROWING METHOD

Planting Plant seeds in spring, into trenches 1 in deep, and thin the seedlings to 14 in apart when they are established. Seeds may also be germinated in seed trays and seedlings transplanted into the garden during the months of spring. Mature plants may be divided in autumn and then replanted in spring. Sow seeds in autumn in hot, dry tropical areas.
Watering Keep chicory well watered during spells of hot weather, especially in hot, dry areas without much natural rainfall.
Fertilizing Add compost to the garden bed in midsummer, but do not provide too much nitrogen or the leaves will grow rapidly at the expense of root growth.
Problems No particular pests or diseases.

CHICORY was probably one of the "bitter herbs" the Israelites ate with the Passover lamb. Christians thought it was an aphrodisiac.

HARVESTING

Picking Pick young green leaves of chicory when they are required.
Storage The leaves cannot be stored either fresh or dried. The root can be dried and then rendered into a powder.
Freezing Not suitable for freezing.

USES

Culinary Use young leaves as soon as they are picked, either in salads or in cooking. The strong, bitterish flavor is similar to dandelion. Flowers can be crystallized and used to decorate cakes and puddings. The root powder is used in beverages.

CHIVES

Allium schoenoprasum, A. tuberosum

GARLIC CHIVES are taller than regular chives and have pretty white flowers.

DAINTY CLUSTERS of mauve flowers and tubular leaves characterize regular chives.

CHINESE CHIVES are eaten as a vegetable in China; here we substitute spring onions.

FEATURES

Chives are perennial herbs that make an attractive edging for a herb garden or bed of mixed annuals and perennials. They grow in clumps from very small bulbs that send up 12 in tall grass-like, hollow, tubular, green leaves, tapering to a point at the top. The plants produce flower stems in summer. The flowers of the common chive, *A. schoenoprasum,* take the form of a dense, globular head of pinkish to pale purple blossoms. Chinese or garlic chives (*A. tuberosum*) have a flower head composed of star-like, white flowers and flat, narrow, light to dark green leaves. Chives can be grown successfully in small containers and clumps can even be potted up and brought indoors to keep in the kitchen.

CONDITIONS

Climate   Chives are very adaptable and can withstand extremes of high and low temperatures. They are frost hardy.

Aspect   Chives grow best in full sun but tolerate partial shade. In very hot, dry climates they may require a little shade and humidity.

Soil   Prepare beds well with organic matter such as compost and bone meal fertilizer. Good drainage is essential. Heavy mulching of the topsoil during summer keeps weeds down and soil moist. For indoor growth, use potting mix and fertilizer.

GROWING METHOD

Planting   Sow seeds directly into the garden during spring. Prepare holes and plant about ten seeds together as a clump, 1/3 in deep. Firm the soil over and water. Keep the soil moist throughout the germination period of 2–3 weeks. Thin out so that the clumps are about 8 in apart. Alternatively, young plants can be raised in seed beds and transplanted into the garden when one month old, again in clumps of ten, 8 in apart. If planting clumps in rows, space the rows 12–24 in apart to allow inter-row cultivation. Bulbs can also be divided in autumn or spring every 2 years once the plant is established. Lift bulbs and break into smaller clumps.

Watering Fertilizing   Water well, especially during hot months. When planting dig in complete plant food. Apply liquid or soluble fertilizer monthly.

Problems   Generally free of diseases but watch for aphids in hot weather. Treat with spray.

BORNE IN LATE SPRING, the flowers make chives one of the most decorative of herbs and a first-rate plant for edging a bed, either in a herb garden or in an old-fashioned cottage garden. Choose plants in flower if possible; some strains are much more richly colored than others.

Picking	Chives are ready to cut when they reach about 6 in high during summer and autumn (autumn to spring in tropical areas). Do not snip off just the tips or the chive will become tough and fibrous. Clip the leaves or blades close to the ground, leaving about 2 in still intact. Harvest chives regularly to keep the crop growing.	
Storage	Chives do not store very well.	
Freezing	Chives can be frozen for about 6 months. Chop them, wrap them in small packages (using plastic wrap), and then freeze them for use when needed at a later date.	

USES

Culinary	Leaves of the chive *A. schoenoprasum* have a delicate, mild onion flavor and are added to soups or casseroles during the last moments of cooking. Chopped leaves are also used in salads, as a garnish over other vegetables and in the French *fines herbes*. The flowers can be eaten fresh, tossed in salads or made into spectacular herb vinegars or butters. All parts of the Chinese chive, *A. tuberosum*, have a mild garlic flavor and the unopened flower bud has a special place in Asian cuisines.

COMFREY
Symphytum officinale

COMFREY LEAVES are handsome but you cannot eat them fresh—they are as rough as sandpaper.

ATTRACTIVE IN GROWTH and in foliage, comfrey makes an unusual tall groundcover. Other species have blue or white flowers.

FEATURES

This large, coarse, hairy perennial grows to 3 ft or more high. It has dark green, lanceolate leaves, which reach 10–12 in long, and clusters of five-lobed flowers in yellow, white or mauve in summer. The sticky qualities of its rhizome, which is black outside and has juicy white flesh within, gave rise to its nickname of slippery root; its other name, knit-bone, comes from its use in healing. The plant dies down over winter but makes a strong recovery in spring and can be quite invasive in the garden, over-running other plants once it takes hold. Confine it to distant parts of the garden where it can form an attractive backdrop.

CONDITIONS

Climate	Prefers moist climates of warm and cool areas. Doesn't grow well in hot, dry, inland areas.
Aspect	Prefers full sun but tolerates partial shade.
Soil	Needs moist, rich soils. Prepare beds with plenty of compost and animal manures.

GROWING METHOD

Planting	Comfrey can be propagated from spring plantings of seed, by cuttings at any stage of its life cycle or by root division in autumn.
Watering	Water well as this fleshy herb requires a great deal of water.
Fertilizing	Requires little fertilizer or other maintenance once established.
Problems	No specific pests or diseases.

Pruning	Cutting the flowers will encourage more leaf growth on this plant.

HARVESTING

Picking	Leaves can be picked in the spring, summer and autumn.
Storage	The leaves can be dried and then stored in airtight containers.
Freezing	Can be frozen for six months.

USES

Culinary	Culinary use is not recommended as controversy surrounds the use of young leaves in salads. Dried leaves are sometimes used to make a herbal tea.
Medicinal	The plant contains unusually high concentrations of vitamin B_{12} but a great deal would need to be eaten daily to have any beneficial effect, and some studies suggest that certain alkaloids in the plant can cause chronic liver problems.
Gardening	Comfrey is best used as a liquid manure: steep fresh leaves in water for several weeks. Leaves can also be used to promote decomposition in the compost heap, and so plant it close by.

CORIANDER
Coriandrum sativum

GROWN AND MUCH LIKED by the ancient Egyptians, Babylonians and Greeks, coriander is also featured in Indian cookery.

FEATURES

Also known as Chinese parsley or cilantro, this very quick-growing, bright green annual reaches a height of approximately 20 in. Leaves on the lower part of the stem are oval with serrated edges but as they mature on the outside branches they become feathery and are divided into narrow segments. The small flowers are white to pink, mauve or reddish and are borne in short-stalked clusters in summer. The spherical seeds are brownish yellow in color, with a diameter of about 1/10 in and they have a musty odor.

CONDITIONS

Climate   Likes hot, dry climates resembling those of the eastern Mediterranean region and southern Europe but will grow in cool, warm and tropical areas.

Aspect   Prefers a sunny position, or partial shade in very hot climates.

Soil   Beds need to be well drained and mulched to keep weed growth down. Coriander is a very fast-growing but short-lived herb which will grow in most soils that are not over-rich in fertilizer. Too much nitrogen lessens the flavor in the plant.

GROWING METHOD

Planting   Successive sowings of seed several weeks apart will extend the harvesting period. Autumn sowings produce seedlings that fare much better than those germinated in spring. Sow directly into garden beds, into holes 1/16 in deep and 8 in apart. Seedlings appear within 1–2 weeks, two from each seed. Thin plants to 4–6 in apart.

Watering   Water evenly and do not let the soil dry out during hot, dry spells.

Fertilizing   No fertilizer is necessary.

Problems   Coriander is prone to bacterial wilt and downy mildew. The mildew may be sprayed; otherwise remove and burn affected plants.

HARVESTING

Picking   Pick fresh leaves as required, the smaller immature leaves having the better taste. Harvest seed when leaves and flowers turn brown and the seed is ripe. Pull out the whole plant, place it upside down in a paper bag and hang it in a cool, dry, airy space. The ripened seeds should fall into the bag.

Storage   Seeds are dried and stored in sealed jars or ground to a powder. The leaves cannot be dried satisfactorily.

Freezing   Leaves can be frozen for up to six months.

USES

Culinary   Leaves, seeds and roots are used for culinary purposes, especially in Asian cuisines. Both leaves and roots can be eaten fresh, the leaves having a pronounced sage flavor with citrus overtones and the roots having an additional nutty flavor. They are also incorporated with meats and vegetables in cooking. Ground coriander seed is much favored as a spice.

CURRY TREE
Murraya koenigii

FEATURES

This small evergreen tree reaches 16 or 20 ft tall and has strongly aromatic, compound leaves which grow to about ½ –2 in long. They are lanceolate to ovate in shape. The small, white flowers are produced during spring and summer in clusters at the ends of the branches and then are followed by dark red berries.

CONDITIONS

Climate A native of India, the curry tree grows best in warm and tropical regions. It tolerates light frosts but only if they are relatively infrequent.

Aspect Prefers full sun but in tropical areas will tolerate shade in the afternoon. In windy areas, grow it in a sheltered spot.

Soil Needs deep, fertile, moisture-retentive soil that drains freely after watering or heavy rain.

GROWING METHOD

Planting Can be raised from seed sown in spring into 6 in wide containers of potting or seed raising mix. When seedlings are about 8 in tall either pot them up to grow bigger or plant them out into their permanent positions. Alternatively, take firm tip cuttings in late spring or early summer. Insert them into sandy potting mix and place the containers onto a heated, seed germinating pad. Keep the soil evenly moist.

Watering Trees grow fastest and best in soils that are always moist, and so give regular, deep soakings if rain is unreliable or during extended droughts.

Fertilizing If soil is deep and fertile, a yearly or twice yearly application of rotted organic matter beneath the foliage canopy will be sufficient. In poorer soils or the tropics, give a ration of complete plant food once in spring and again towards the end of summer.

Problems No particular problems.

Pruning No pruning is necessary but the tree can be pruned at the start of spring in order to control its size.

THIS YOUNG CURRY TREE will eventually reach about 20 ft tall. The leaves are fried until crisp before they are added to curries.

HARVESTING

Picking The leaves can be harvested at any time as they are needed.

Storage Leaves can be dried but this diminishes the flavor and the longer they are stored the less flavor there will be.

Freezing Not suitable for freezing.

USES

Culinary Fresh leaves are used to impart a curry-like flavor to soups, stews, pickles and marinades. They cannot be used as a substitute for curry powder which is a different product altogether.

Medicinal In India, all parts of the tree are used medicinally. Extracts are said to be effective for the relief of headaches, diarrhea and intestinal worms.

Gardening This attractive tree infuses the garden with its spicy aroma. It can also be grown successfully in a big tub.

DANDELION
Taraxacum officinale

FEATURES

A perennial flower often seen as a weed in lawns or neglected places, dandelion produces a flat rosette of deeply lobed, bright green leaves from a big, fleshy taproot. Bright yellow flowers are produced in spring and summer on hollow, leafless stems and develop into puffy, spherical seed heads that shatter when ripe, the individual seeds floating away on the breeze. Dandelion has a milky sap and its hollow flower stems differentiate it from other weeds.

CONDITIONS

Climate   Grows best in cool to warm climates, especially the higher rainfall areas. Not well suited to tropical regions.

Aspect   Full sun is essential.

Soil   Not particularly fussy as to soil but you will get the biggest and best roots and less bitter leaves by growing plants in good quality, friable, well-drained soil.

GROWING METHOD

Planting   Sow seeds in spring directly where the plants are to grow, with a bed in an established vegetable patch being the most suitable site. Plants may also be grown in containers that are deeper than they are wide so as to accommodate the long taproot. Although they are perennials, individual dandelion plants should be dug and discarded every two or three years. Replace them with fresh seedlings.

Watering   Keep the soil evenly moist.

Fertilizing   Avoid excessive fertilizing. If plants are grown in a bed that has had rotted manure dug into it, no further fertilizing is required. For container growth, incorporate controlled release fertilizer into the potting mix at planting time and feed the growing plants monthly with liquid or soluble fertilizer.

Problems   No particular problems.

Pruning   Remove flower stems as they rise or, if the pretty flowers are wanted, deadhead as they fade to stop unwanted seed formation. If seed heads are allowed to ripen, dandelion becomes an invasive weed.

DANDELIONS are often considered a weed, but the yellow flowers are very pretty and the leaves are full of vitamins.

HARVESTING

Picking   Fresh spring leaves can be picked while small and sweet. Bigger, older leaves are very bitter. Bitterness can be reduced by blanching, that is, excluding light. Do this by covering the plant with an upturned tin or flower pot, being sure that all holes are covered. Young leaves are ready for picking when they have lost all or most of their green color. Harvest roots only in late autumn or winter or they will lack flavor and body.

Storage   Leaves must be used fresh but roots are stored by first roasting them and then grinding the results into an airtight jar.

Freezing   Roasted, ground roots will stay fresher and more flavorsome if stored in the freezer like fresh coffee.

USES

Culinary   Young, sweet leaves are highly nutritious and can be used in salads, stir fries or to make teas. The roots, which are cleaned, chopped and roasted until dark brown, are ground and used as a coffee substitute.

Medicinal   The sticky, white sap of the dandelion is used to remove warts. Dandelion coffee is sleep inducing and a detoxicant said to be good for the kidneys and liver.

DILL
Anethum graveolens

FEATURES

An annual herb growing to 3 ft, dill looks very like fennel, with its threadlike, feathery, blue-green leaves. It has a single, thin taproot rising above the ground to form a long, hollow stalk. This stalk branches at the top to support a 6 in wide mass of small, yellow flowers, appearing in clusters, in summer. Flat, oval seeds, brown in color, are produced quickly and in great quantities.

CONDITIONS

Climate Needs a warmish, dry summer but can be grown with some success in cooler regions that are frost free.

Aspect Prefers full sun; may need support and protection from winds.

Soil Dig plenty of organic matter into the garden beds so as to improve water retention, as these plants mature through the drier months of spring and summer.

GROWING METHOD

Planting Plant dill by seed anytime except during winter. Dill will quite often self-sow and so choose a permanent position for the initial plantings. Successive planting every two weeks is recommended to ensure that there is continuous harvest. Sow the seeds in shallow furrows, with at least 2 ft between the rows, and then thin the seedlings out to 1 ft apart when they have reached approximately 2 in in height.

Watering Keep the plants well watered, especially during hot weather.

Fertilizing Mulch well throughout spring and summer with rotted organic matter such as compost or old manure.

Problems No particular damaging pests or diseases affect this plant.

HARVESTING

Picking Dill leaves can be picked within 2 months of planting. Clip close to the stem in the cooler parts of the day. Several weeks after the plant blossoms, pick the flower heads and place them in a paper bag—store in a cool, dry place until seeds ripen—or stems can be cut and hung upside down until seeds ripen and fall.

THE FEATHERY LEAVES and greenish-yellow flowers of dill make a graceful summer picture. The flowers are used in making spiced olives.

Storage Leaves and stems can be frozen and pieces cut off as required. They do not keep for more than a couple of days in the refrigerator before drooping and losing flavor. Dry leaves by spreading them thinly over a firm, non-metallic surface in a warm, dark place. After drying, place them in an airtight container. Seeds are dried in a similar manner.

Freezing Leaves can be frozen for up to 6 months.

USES

Culinary Dill has a pronounced tang. Fresh leaves are used in salads and as a garnish. The seeds are used ground or whole in cooked dishes, as well as in the making of vinegars, pickles and herb butters. Dried leaves are often added to soups or sauces. It is a great favorite in fish dishes. Tea can be made from the seeds.

Gardening Dill is considered an ideal companion plant for lettuce, cabbage and onions.

ELDER
Sambucus nigra

FEATURES

A deciduous shrub or small tree, elder or elderberry is usually less than 32 ft tall with rough, corky bark and compound leaves composed of five or so toothed, dark green leaflets. Heads of creamy white, scented flowers appear in summer leading to shiny, blue-black berries in autumn. The flowers attract bees while the berries are eaten by birds. Where autumn nights are sufficiently cold, elder leaves color well before falling.

CONDITIONS

Climate Best in cool climates. Grows well enough in warm areas but does not produce much in the way of autumn color there.

Aspect A sunny position is best although the plant will tolerate bright, dappled shade or a few hours of full shade each day.

Soil Friable, fertile soil that drains well yet stays moist is best, but elder accepts a wide range of soil types.

GROWING METHOD

Planting Plants can be grown from seed sown in spring, or suckers, with their own roots, can be dug and detached from the parent plant. This can be done at any time but spring is probably best. Elders can also be propagated by cuttings. Take hardwood cuttings in winter or tip cuttings in spring. Root either type in containers of very sandy potting mix. Pot them up to grow larger and then plant out into their permanent position. If you are planting a group or row, leave at least 10 ft between each to allow room for the suckers to develop.

Watering Elders like moisture at their roots at all times, especially in hot, dry weather in summer. If rainfall is reliable and reasonably regular, mature plants usually need little extra water.

Fertilizing In average garden soils no special fertilizing is required, especially if you mulch beneath the plants with rotted organic matter. If soil is not particularly fertile, a ration of complete plant food once in early spring is sufficient.

Problems No particular problems.

Pruning No pruning is necessary.

THE CREAMY-WHITE FLOWERS of the elder are heavily scented. They appear in clusters during early summer.

HARVESTING

Picking Flower heads are picked in the morning but only when all the flowers on each head have bloomed. Dry them in a cool, dark, airy place. Berries are picked when ripe.

Storage Dried flowers can be removed from their stems and stored in airtight containers. Ripe berries can also be dried and similarly stored.

Freezing Berries that have been cooked for a few minutes may be frozen for later use.

USES

Cosmetic Cold elderflower tea splashed onto the face daily tones and soothes the skin and is good for the complexion generally.

Culinary Fresh flowers are made into elderflower wine and jams and jellies. The berries can also be made into jams or jellies and the juice can be fermented into elderberry wine. Berries should not be eaten raw.

Medicinal Tea made from young leaves and taken in small doses is a diuretic, while the juice of cooked berries is taken for headaches.

Gardening Elderberries, with their dense growth and suckering habit, make a good privacy screen and reasonable windbreak. Use as an understorey shrub beneath tall, open trees.

EVENING PRIMROSE
Oenothera biennis

FEATURES

Evening primrose is an annual flower with many upright, leafy stems. From late spring and right through the summer, each of these stems is topped with a cluster of golden yellow, sweetly fragrant flowers which open towards the end of the day. The foliage, which is bluish-green, forms a rosette around the base of the plant. Evening primrose is native to dry areas in the central and eastern United States. It should be planted with caution as it self-seeds most prolifically and can spread fast in favored locations.

CONDITIONS

Climate Grows in cool, warm and hot, arid places.
Aspect Full sun is essential.
Soil Not very fussy about soil and grows in most places so long as the drainage is good. This plant thrives in average garden soils.

GROWING METHOD

Planting Grows from seed sown in autumn or early spring directly where it is to grow. Thin seedlings out so that there is at least 12 in between each.
Watering Do not overwater. Once established, plants are drought tolerant and can usually get by on rain in areas where it falls regularly.
Fertilizing No fertilizing is necessary. Over-rich soils can lead to excessive foliage growth and weak or deformed stems.
Problems No particular problems.
Pruning Pruning is not necessary but snap off flower stems after the blooms have faded but before the seeds ripen. This plant self-seeds freely and can create a major weed problem. Allow one plant to seed in order to regenerate the plants but collect the seed before it falls so that you can sow it where you want it.

HARVESTING

Picking All parts of the plant are edible. Leaves may be picked anytime while seeds are harvested when ripe in autumn. The small roots may also be dug in spring or autumn.
Storage Seeds are stored in airtight containers. Other parts of the plant are used fresh.
Freezing Not suitable for freezing.

EVENING PRIMROSE earns its name by blooming only at dusk. There are perennial species that keep their blooms open all day.

USES

Culinary Fresh leaves are used in salads or can be lightly steamed or stir fried. Seeds can be eaten raw or used in recipes.
Medicinal Tea made from the leaves is good for coughs and colds and is a tonic for the liver, kidneys and intestines. An oil contained in the seeds has traditionally been credited with amazing therapeutic powers.
Gardening Evening primrose is a pretty plant and a good partner for other meadow flowers such as California poppies and paper daisies.

FENNEL

Foeniculum vulgare

FEATURES

Fast growing and spreading, this herbaceous perennial can reach a height of nearly 6 ft. An erect, finely foliaged plant with a strong aniseed aroma, it has a bulbous, fleshy base, hollow stems and delicate, thread-like, dark olive green leaves. Flattened heads of tiny, bright yellow flowers appear on the top of the plant in spring. Fennel is an extremely invasive plant that has been declared a noxious weed in some areas. It should only be grown where unwanted spread can be easily controlled.

CONDITIONS

Climate   Very tough and adaptable, fennel grows in most areas but does best in cool to warm climates where frosts are not very severe. It is not well suited to the high levels of summer rain and humidity in the tropics.

Aspect   Full sun is essential and shelter from blustery winds advisable.

Soil   Grows on a wide variety of soils but is most vigorous on crumbly, sandy loam with plenty of rotted organic matter. Dig in a cupful of lime per square yard of soil before planting as fennel prefers slightly alkaline conditions.

GROWING METHOD

Planting   Most easily grown from seed sown in spring or, in frost-free areas, autumn. Sow the seeds directly where they are to grow, 1/5 in deep and about 12 in apart. Vigorous young plants produce the sweetest and best flavored "bulbs" and you should dig out and replace plants every three years.

Watering   Keep well watered during spring and summer. Consistent moisture around the roots ensures sweet, succulent growth. From about mid-autumn, let the rain do the watering unless your winters are very dry.

Fertilizing   Additional feeding is not necessary if soil is rich and fertile. If in doubt, apply complete plant food once in early spring.

Problems   No particular problems.

VERSATILE FENNEL has many culinary uses: the fleshy base is eaten as a vegetable, and seeds and leaves add flavor to other dishes.

HARVESTING

Picking   Pick leaves anytime from late spring to late summer. Seeds are harvested when ripe in late summer and as this time approaches, plants should be inspected regularly so that ripe seeds can be gathered before they start to fall. The bulbous bases can be dug as required.

Storage   Dried seeds are stored in airtight jars. Use the leaves fresh as they lose flavor during drying.

Freezing   Wrap small bunches of leaves in a freezer bag or foil and freeze for up to 6 months.

USES

Cosmetic   Cold tea made from the seeds is a refreshing facial rinse that is said to reduce wrinkles and tone the skin.

Culinary   Seeds, which are an aid to digestion, are chewed raw or used whole or ground in recipes. Finely chopped leaves are added to many dishes, notably fish and carbohydrates such as pasta and potatoes, and to vinegars. The fleshy, white base is eaten raw or cooked.

Medicinal   All parts of fennel are said to be beneficial to the digestion, good for the eyes and a mild appetite suppressant. Tea made from the seeds is a mild laxative. Chewing the seeds freshens stale breath.

FEVERFEW

Tanacetum parthenium, syn. *Chrysanthemum parthenium*

FEATURES

A perennial flower, feverfew has aromatic, finely cut leaves and clusters of small, white daisy-like flowers in spring (summer in cool areas). The plant is densely foliaged and can grow to nearly 3 ft tall. Leaves are usually a fresh, light green but a golden-foliaged form is also sold.

CONDITIONS

Climate Best in cool to warm areas but grows in the tropics as an annual in cooler, drier months.

Aspect Full sun is essential in cooler areas. In warmer districts feverfew prefers light shade on summer afternoons but plants will grow lax and flower poorly in areas that are too shady.

Soil Average, well-drained garden soil is all that is needed. In over-rich soils plants produce too much soft, leafy growth.

GROWING METHOD

Planting Easily grown from seed sown in early spring. Press seeds just beneath the surface where the plants are to grow. Established plants can be dug up in winter and divided into several new plants. Each division should have its own roots and the divisions should be replanted immediately. Soft-tip cuttings taken in mid-spring will also root easily. Make cuttings about 3 in long and insert them into small pots of very sandy potting mix. Place in a warm but shady and sheltered spot and keep moist. Roots should form in about 3 weeks.

Watering Do not overwater. Feverfew does not thrive on neglect but does not need frequent watering. Overwet conditions will cause the plant to rot.

Fertilizing A ration of complete plant food applied once each spring will meet the plant's needs. Alternatively, feed monthly with liquid or soluble plant food and water in.

Problems Slugs, snails and caterpillars can strip the foliage or eat young plants entirely. Lay snail bait during spring and autumn; pick off and squash caterpillars when seen. For major infestations of caterpillars spray plants with products containing *Bacillus thuringiensis*, a biological control that affects only caterpillars.

FOR THE HERB GARDEN, most people prefer this single, daisy-like feverfew but there is also a very pretty double white one.

HARVESTING

Picking All the upper parts of the plant are useful medicinally and whole plants may be harvested anytime they are in full bloom. Fresh, young leaves can be harvested anytime but remember that plants need their leaves to live and you should grow enough plants so that picking is not concentrated on just one or two.

Storage Dry upper parts, including leaves, stems and flowers, in a cool, dark, airy place. When dry, coarsely chop and store in an airtight jar.

Freezing Freshly picked leaves can be wrapped in foil and frozen, for up to 6 months, for later use.

USES

Cosmetic Feverfew makes a useful moisturiser.

Medicinal Tea made from the dried upper parts is drunk to relieve indigestion and period pain. Eating one or two fresh leaves every day may help prevent the onset of migraines in sufferers but in some people this causes mouth ulcers.

Craft Flower stems placed in linen closets will discourage moths.

Gardening Feverfew is attractive and gives a good display when plants are massed together or used to border paths. It attracts bees and is often planted near fruit trees to assist pollination.

GALANGAL
Alpinia galanga

FEATURES

A member of the ginger family, this perennial forms a clump of leafy stems up to 6 ft tall. Leaves are glossy and light green, about 20 in long and lanceolate in shape. Unremarkable flowers appear in summer and autumn and are followed by spherical, red fruits. The plant is native to tropical southeast Asia. It can be grown in large containers.

CONDITIONS

Climate   Best in tropical areas but grows satisfactorily, if a little slowly, anywhere frost free. Where winters are cold but summers long and hot, try planting after the last frost in winter or spring and lifting after the first frost of autumn.

Aspect   Takes bright dappled sun or part shade in the tropics but needs full sun and a warm, sheltered position elsewhere.

Soil   Best in deep, fertile, free-draining soil with plenty of rotted organic matter. Roots rot in wet soil. Use top quality potting mix for pots.

GROWING METHOD

Planting   Plant sections of fresh rhizome bought in spring from an Asian grocery store or good fruit market. Cut the rhizome into sections about 3 in long, each with an obvious green growing tip. Allow the cut ends to dry for a few days and then plant horizontally 3–4 in below the surface and water in.
Alternatively, lift an existing plant in late winter and replant some of the rhizomes as above. Growing from seed takes much more time. Sow the seeds into trays of seed-raising mix. Cover lightly, moisten and place on a heated seed germinating pad in a bright, warm place. Keep moist and when seedlings are big enough to handle, prick out into individual containers. Plant out when at least 6 in tall.

Watering   Keep plants well watered from the time growth appears in spring until autumn when the top growth begins to die back. These plants are from rainy, tropical areas and expect a lot of rain in summer. Plants in pots may need watering every day during the hotter periods of summer.

GALANGAL RHIZOMES resemble those of their cousin, the ginger, and they are used in the same way. They have a sharper, "hotter" taste.

Fertilizing   Apply a complete plant food at planting time or when growth begins, and then feed the plant each month with liquid or soluble plant food. Mulch around the plants with rotted manure. Potted galangal should be fed biweekly with liquid or soluble fertilizer and it is a good idea to mix a tablespoon of controlled release fertilizer into the potting mix at planting time.

Problems   No particular problems.

HARVESTING

Picking   Galangal is usually lifted in autumn when the leaves begin to deteriorate. The rhizomes are detached for culinary use with one or two being replanted for next year's crop.

Storage   Cleaned rhizomes may be stored in the crisper bin of the refrigerator for a few weeks. They can also be pickled for long-term storage and they keep reasonably well in a cool, dark, well-ventilated cupboard.

Freezing   Freeze until needed then grate while still frozen.

USES

Culinary   Reminiscent of ginger but with a distinctly different flavor, galangal (also known as Laos powder) is a popular addition to many dishes of Indonesian, Thai and Malaysian origin.

GARLIC
Allium sativum

FEATURES

Garlic grows from a bulb that consists of several segments, the strongly aromatic cloves that have led to its widespread culinary use. This perennial plant also has a long list of medicinal uses. Its erect, gray-green leaves stand about 2 ft tall, sometimes taller. Nondescript white flowers appear in summer, after which the leaves die back and the plant enters its annual winter dormancy.

CONDITIONS

Climate This very adaptable plant grows well in a wide range of climates, but it dislikes the high summer heat, humidity and rainfall of the tropics. There it can be grown in deep pots of sandy potting mix if sheltered from constant rain. Even so, the results may be disappointing.

Aspect Full sun is essential.

Soil Good drainage is essential but garlic grows in any crumbly, reasonably fertile soil. Dark, sandy loam with rotted organic matter and a cupful of lime per square yard is ideal.

GROWING METHOD

Planting At mid-autumn or in early spring, break cloves from a fresh garlic bought at the food store. Push into soil that is well dug over and crumbly so that the pointy end is ¼ –½ in below the surface. Space cloves about 8 in apart, cover with soil and water in well. Mulch lightly with compost, rotted manure or rotted grass clippings.

Watering Newly planted garlic needs moisture for its developing roots but does not want to be soaked during autumn and winter. If rain does not fall, water deeply once a week. Gradually reduce watering as the weather warms up in spring as garlic needs a hot, dry summer to mature the bulbs.

Fertilizing If garlic is grown in deep, fertile soil, an application of complete plant food at planting time is all the fertilizer needed.

Problems Aphids may cluster on leaves and flower buds but are easily rubbed off by hand. Bad drainage or overwatering causes bulbs to rot.

THE PRINCE OF SEASONERS, garlic has a long history of use in medicine and magic, especially as protection against witchcraft.

HARVESTING

Picking Harvest garlic in autumn or summer if the leaves have yellowed. Don't cut the dead leaves off—use them to plait the bulbs together for storage. After harvest, wash the bulbs clean and then leave in the sun for a few days to dry.

Storage Dried bulbs may be strung together and hung in a dry, airy place for use as needed.

Freezing Not suitable for freezing.

USES

Culinary Garlic has hundreds of uses in virtually every type of cuisine. It is an essential ingredient in many European and Asian dishes, and it is used in vinegars and herb butters. The leaves can be chopped into salads or lightly stir fried.

Medicinal Garlic has antibiotic and antiseptic properties and is one of the most widely taken medicinal herbs. It is useful in lowering both blood pressure and cholesterol and is said to have beneficial effects on the immune system. Regular intake of garlic reduces susceptibility to colds and improves the digestive system. A sliced clove rubbed over cuts will clean and sterilize the wound.

Gardening Garlic is often planted under roses as it is believed to improve their growth and help deter aphids and other rose pests.

GINGER

Zingiber officinale

FEATURES

A clump-forming perennial, ginger is a native of tropical lowland rainforests. It has many erect stems that grow to about 4 ft tall. Lanceolate leaves, medium green and about 8 in long, are produced all along the stems. Not very showy flowers appear in summer after which the top growth begins to die back.

CONDITIONS

Climate   A tropical climate is best but ginger will grow anywhere frost free.

Aspect   In the tropics, part or dappled shade is best. In warm areas more sun is needed but ginger still appreciates shade on hot summer afternoons. Shelter from strong winds is essential.

Soil   For best results grow in deep, friable, well-drained soil that is rich in rotted organic matter and a little on the alkaline side (dig in a cup of lime to the square yard at planting time). Ginger is a heavy feeder and you should prepare the planting site well. Dig the bed over deeply, adding rotted manure or compost and complete plant food as you go. The finished bed should be light, fine and crumbly.

GROWING METHOD

Planting   Plants can be started from sections of fresh root ginger bought at the grocery store. Cut the rhizome in sections about 3 in long, ensuring that each has a pointed growth bud. Allow the cut ends to dry for a few days before planting horizontally 3–4 in below the surface. Water in thoroughly. In tropical areas plant in autumn but otherwise mid-spring is better. Mulch the planted bed with compost, rotted manure, salt hay or other old organic matter. Don't plant the rhizomes too closely together, especially in the tropics, as ginger is a spreading plant that needs space.

Watering   At planting time, water in deeply. In tropical areas where winters are dry, continue to water deeply once a week. In other climates, keep the soil lightly moist, gradually increasing the water as temperatures rise. In summer, the plant cannot be overwatered if drainage is good. After the plant has flowered, start to reduce the watering.

THE GLOSSY LEAVES of ginger have a warm, spicy aroma. It used to be believed tigers would run away if it was waved at them.

Fertilizing   As well as the fertilizer applied at planting time, ginger should be fed with liquid or soluble plant food monthly from mid-spring to late summer. Replacing the mulch as it is washed into the soil also helps feed the plant.

Problems   No particular problems.

Pruning   In autumn, old stems can be cut out at ground level to make room for vigorous new growth.

HARVESTING

Picking   Ginger is harvested in autumn. Dig up and detach the rhizomes, replanting a few to produce next year's crop.

Storage   Rhizomes can be stored in the crisper bin of the refrigerator for a few weeks or may be pickled or crystallized for long-term storage.

Freezing   Freeze rhizomes until needed, then grate while still frozen.

USES

Culinary   Ginger is widely used in Asian, African and Caribbean cuisine. It is an essential ingredient in everything from curries, soups and stews to salads and vegetable dishes. Crystallized, it is enjoyed as a sweet; dried, powdered ginger is added to cakes, biscuits and other foods.

Medicinal   Fresh juice directly applied is said to relieve the pain of burns.

HERB ROBERT
Geranium robertianum

FEATURES

A biennial herb, often grown as an annual, herb Robert may reach a height of 12 in. It has deeply lobed, toothed leaves which sometimes develop a reddish cast. Pinkish flowers appear in spring in airy clusters. In the wild, the plant is widely distributed in temperate parts of the northern hemisphere. Explosive seed capsules make the plant potentially invasive where conditions suit it.

CONDITIONS

Climate Most suited to cool climates but will grow reasonably well in warm areas. As plants die back in winter they will withstand frosts.

Aspect Full sun or part shade are equally suitable.

Soil Not particularly fussy about soil types as long as they drain freely. Average garden soil is quite satisfactory.

GROWING METHOD

Planting Can be grown from seed saved from last year and sown shallowly in spring or take cuttings of basal shoots in middle to late spring. Make cuttings about 3 in long and insert them into small pots of very sandy potting mix. Keep lightly moist in a warm, bright, but shaded place. Roots should form within a month and the new plants can either be placed in the garden or potted up to grow bigger.

Watering Herb Robert does not need a lot of water and in places where summers are mild regular rainfall can be sufficient. If watering is necessary, water deeply once a week rather than giving more frequent light sprinklings.

Fertilizing In garden beds that are mulched regularly with rotted organic matter, no further fertilizer is needed. Elsewhere, a ration of complete plant food applied once during spring is enough.

Problems The fungus disease rust, which attacks all plants of the *Geranium* and *Pelargonium* families, can disfigure the foliage and weaken the plant. It appears as yellow spots on the upper surface of the leaf with raised lumps of "rust" underneath. Rust occurs mainly during warm, humid weather. To control it, either pick off affected leaves at the first sign of infection or spray the plant with a fungicide suitable for the condition (the label will tell you). Don't drop or compost any of the affected leaves. They should be burned or placed into the garbage bin.

HERB ROBERT has one of those scents you either like or loathe. It is said to be named after St Robert who discovered its medicinal qualities.

HARVESTING

Picking Leaves are used fresh and may be picked at any time as required.

Storage Not usually stored.

Freezing Not suitable for freezing.

USES

Medicinal Traditionally, herb Robert has been used to treat a range of complaints as varied as toothache and conjunctivitis.

Gardening The plant is pretty enough in its own right and makes a good addition to a planting of mixed flowers. It is a good understorey plant beneath open foliaged trees.

HOREHOUND
Marrubium vulgare

FEATURES

From the Mediterranean region, horehound is a perennial with sprawling branches. It grows to a height of around 20 in, sometimes more. The rough-textured, gray-green leaves are roundish and somewhat downy, especially when young. They have a strong aroma and are very bitter to taste. Dense, spherical heads of white flowers appear in summer and after bloom these dry to become stiff and spiky. Horehound is regarded as a noxious plant in some areas: check with your extension service before planting it.

CONDITIONS

Climate Best suited to cool and warm regions, especially those where winters are rainy.
Aspect Full sun is essential.
Soil Grows in a wide range of soil types if drainage is good. Plants rot if soil stays wet in winter.

GROWING METHOD

Planting Most easily raised from softwood cuttings taken from new growth in spring or early autumn. Root the cuttings in pots of sandy potting mix kept shaded and moist. Mature, well-established plants may be dug up in late winter and divided into several smaller plants. Seeds saved from last year's flowers can also be used to start the plant. Sow them from middle to late spring where they are to grow. Thin seedlings to about 12 in apart.
Watering In the wild, horehound receives most of its rain from about mid-autumn to about mid-spring with much less during the summer. In the garden, simulate these conditions by watering during the cooler half of the year—a deep soaking once a week is plenty. Taper off watering as summer approaches, giving the odd deep soaking only.
Fertilizing Plants occur naturally in areas with dry, poor soils and in average garden conditions will not need any additional fertilizer.
Problems No particular problems as far as pests or diseases are concerned but the plant can be spread widely by seed. Prevent this by removing the flower heads immediately after they have finished blooming.
Pruning If plants are looking tattered by the end of autumn they may be cut to ground level. New growth will appear in spring.

HOREHOUND has been used to alleviate coughs and colds since the days of the ancient Egyptians. It has a place in any historical garden.

HARVESTING

Picking Leaves to be used fresh can be picked anytime. Stems of flowers and leaves that are to be dried should be picked in the morning.
Storage Stems of dried flowers and leaves can be stored in airtight jars. Tie bunches of flowers and leaves together and hang them upside down in a dry, airy place. When they are dry, crumble into containers.
Freezing Not suitable for freezing.

USES

Culinary Leaves can be boiled with sugar and water to make candied horehound, and they can also be used to give a bitter flavor to homebrew beer.
Medicinal Horehound tea, an infusion made from the leaves, stems and flowers, is taken for coughs and colds and as a gentle laxative. Horehound is a diuretic and may be taken to help relieve kidney problems.

HORSERADISH
Armoracia rusticana

FEATURES

Although it is a perennial plant, horseradish is often grown as an annual. It is a rather weedy looking plant, consisting as it does of a clump of big, soft, spinach-like leaves, and it is best grown tucked away in the vegetable patch. In spring a stem of unremarkable, off-white flowers rises from the center of the clump.

CONDITIONS

Climate Cool and warm climates are most suitable.
Aspect Full sun is essential.
Soil Grow in deep soil that has been dug over deeply—a vegetable patch is ideal. This plant enjoys good conditions and thrives in well-drained soils that are rich in rotted manure.

GROWING METHOD

Planting The entire root system may be dug up in late autumn and replanted in spring to control the plant's ability to spread rapidly. New plants are introduced into the garden as root cuttings. In mild areas they may be planted in autumn but where winters are severe, spring planting is better. Allow about 14 in between each plant. The following autumn, take 8–10 in cuttings of the straight, thin side roots. These may be replanted immediately in mild areas but in cold places they are best kept over winter in just-damp sphagnum moss, soil or sand. Replant in spring.

Watering Keep horseradish moist during spring and summer. If grown in the vegetable patch, give it the same watering as the other vegetables.

Fertilizing Mix a ration of low nitrogen fertilizer into the planting hole and drench two or three times during the growing season with a low nitrogen liquid or soluble plant food—one designed to promote flowering is ideal. Too much nitrogen makes too many leaves and poor quality roots.

Problems Snails, slugs and caterpillars are all drawn to the fleshy leaves and will strip young plants quickly if not controlled. Lay bait for snails and slugs and either pick off and squash caterpillars or spray plants with preparations containing *Bacillus thuringiensis*, a biological control that kills only caterpillars.

HORSERADISH ROOTS are made into a piquant sauce for roast beef. In France they are sometimes eaten raw to stimulate the appetite.

HARVESTING

Picking Main harvest is in autumn although side roots can be snipped off in summer for immediate use. Do this by scraping soil away from the main root, replacing it when the desired roots have been cut. For the main harvest, lift the plant, ensuring that all roots are removed (or the plant will regrow). Use selected side roots for regeneration, the rest for processing.

Storage Fresh whole roots can be stored in the refrigerator for about two weeks while the grated roots can be made into horseradish sauce or pickled in vinegar.

Freezing Whole roots can be wrapped in foil and frozen for up to 6 months.

USES

Culinary Horseradish sauce is a popular condiment with beef but can also be served with other meats and fish. It can be added sparingly to sauces and salad dressings.

Medicinal Horseradish is an instant remedy for blocked noses but is not an easy medicine to take. It has antiseptic properties and is said to ward off colds if small amounts are eaten regularly. It is highly nutritious, containing high amounts of vitamin C and many essential minerals.

HYSSOP

Hyssopus officinalis

FEATURES

A perennial to around 2 ft tall, hyssop has many erect stems clothed in narrow, lanceolate, sage green leaves. Spikes of small flowers appear on top of each stem in summer. Usually these flowers are blue-violet but they may also be pink or white. The whole plant exudes a pungent aroma and the leaves have a bitter taste.

CONDITIONS

Climate   Best in cool or warm areas. Possible in the tropics if grown in pots sheltered from heavy summer rains.

Aspect   Full sun produces compact growth and the strongest flavor but hyssop tolerates shade for part of the day.

Soil   Likes light, fertile, well-drained soils but will grow in any reasonably fertile soil as long as it drains freely.

GROWING METHOD

Planting   Hyssop can be grown from seed, softwood cuttings or division of the roots. Sow seeds in spring into trays of seed-raising mix. Cover lightly, keep moist and when seedlings are big enough to handle prick out into small, individual pots to grow on. Plant out about 12 in apart when plants are about 8 in tall. Take 3 in tip cuttings in spring and insert into pots of sandy potting mix. Keep the mix moist and in bright, sheltered shade and roots will form within a month. To divide, lift an established plant in late autumn or early spring. Cut the root mass into several smaller sections, each with its own roots. Replant the sections immediately.

Watering   Keep soil moist, especially during the warmer months but do not overwater. Hyssop is a resilient plant that can often get by on rain.

Fertilizing   A ration of complete plant food applied once in spring when new growth appears is enough.

Problems   No particular problems.

Pruning   When new growth begins in spring, pinching out the tips of young stems will encourage the plant to become more bushy and thus produce more flowers. In late autumn, the remains of the plant can be cut to ground level.

THE RICH BLUE FLOWERS of hyssop adorn the garden in spring, and they are much loved by bees who make superb honey from them.

HARVESTING

Picking   Flowers for using fresh or for drying are picked when in full bloom and individual stems can be harvested as needed.

Storage   Store flowers and leaves dry. Cut bunches of flowering stems, tie them together and hang them upside down in a dim, airy place. When they are dry, crumble them into airtight jars.

Freezing   Not suitable for freezing.

USES

Cosmetic   Oil distilled from hyssop is used in perfumes and other commercial cosmetics. At home, it may be added to bath water, and cooled hyssop leaf tea is a cleansing, refreshing facial rinse.

Culinary   One or two fresh leaves, finely chopped and added late, give an appealing piquancy to soups and casseroles while fresh flowers can be used to add flavor and color to salads.

Medicinal   Tea, made by infusing the dried stems, leaves and flowers in boiling water, is taken to relieve the symptoms of colds; hyssop leaves are often a component in mixed herbal tonics and teas.

Gardening   Hyssop is a decorative plant and very attractive to bees and butterflies. Use it in a border of mixed flowers or grow it as an edging to paths.

LAVENDER
Lavandula

FEATURES

The many varieties of this fragrant perennial herb include *L. angustifolia* (a favorite subspecies is *L. angustifolia* 'Alba,' white lavender), *L. dentata* and *L. stoechas*. The common names English, French and Italian lavender are used but authorities disagree which species is which. Heights differ but all grow into evergreen, bushy shrubs with woody stems and hairy, silvery to gray-green, fragrant leaves. Edges are smooth or serrated, depending on variety. Long spikes of fragrant deep purple to pinkish flowers appear in late winter to spring, sometimes in summer.

CONDITIONS

Climate Best suited to cool or warm climates where most rain falls in winter. Not suited to the tropics or very humid areas.

Aspect Prefers full sun. Flowering spikes need protection from severe winds.

Soil Prefers well-drained soil, but it need not be rich. If it is acid, add lime or dolomite.

GROWING METHOD

Planting Seed has a long germination time and may not come true to strain: taking cuttings is the best way to get the lavender you want. Take 2 in tip cuttings with a heel or base of old wood in autumn or late winter. Trim off upper and lower leaves and plant in a mixture of two-thirds coarse sand to one-third peat moss. Keep soil on the dry side until the cutting has taken root and new leaf shoots appear. Then pot on into a good quality potting mix. Plant in the garden in spring 5–6 ft apart. Or pull a lower branch of a mature plant to soil level, slightly scratch the underside and peg it into the soil. Once the branch has taken root, cut it off and transfer it to its new spot.

Watering Water only in dry weather as lavenders do not require a great deal of water.

Fertilizing Applications of a complete fertilizer NPK 5:6:7 will improve fragrance. Less cold-resistant varieties may need mulching in the winter.

ENGLISH LAVENDER is distinguished from the dumpier French, Italian and Spanish types by its slender flower spikes.

Problems Roots are often attacked in this otherwise tough plant. Root-knot nematodes can arrest the flow of nutrients and water to the plant. Companion planting with marigolds will keep nematodes down. Root rot can result from poor drainage and diseased plants need to be removed. Leaf spot, causing yellowing leaves with whitish spots, indicates plants may be too close together and need more air circulation. Do not water over leaves.

Pruning Keep plants pruned in their first year to discourage flowering: bushier plants result.

HARVESTING

Picking Flowers can be cut in early spring before they open. Dry by hanging in bunches in a dry, airy, hot place.

Storage Store dried leaves and flowers in airtight jars.

Freezing Not suitable for freezing.

USES

Culinary Fresh or dried flowers and leaves are used to flavor sugars, jellies, ice cream and cheeses. Flowers can also be crystallized and used as decoration on cakes.

Craft Dried lavender spikes are used for their fragrance in potpourris, perfumed sachets and dried arrangements. Lavender is also used to make essential oil and floral waters.

LAVENDER COTTON
Santolina chamaecyparissus

FEATURES

Gray, rounded and cushiony, lavender cotton is a low, groundcovering shrub that usually grows about 12 in tall, sometimes taller. When crushed, the toothed leaves give off a strong aroma reminiscent of lavender but with a delightful difference. In summer, dull yellow flowers appear on leafless stems and make a striking contrast to the soft gray leaves.

CONDITIONS

Climate Originally from the Mediterranean region, lavender cotton suits both cool and warm climates and tolerates the heat of arid areas if watered as needed.

Aspect Full sun is essential.

Soil Good drainage is essential but, given that, lavender cotton grows well in poor, rather dry soils. If conditions are too rich it loses its dense, compact appearance and becomes straggly and lax. This plant will tolerate alkaline soils.

GROWING METHOD

Planting In late spring, take 3 in long cuttings of stems that have lost their sappy freshness but have not yet become woody. Insert the cuttings into small containers of sandy potting mix, keep the mix moist and the container shaded until roots develop after 4–6 weeks. Harden off the cuttings by moving the container into full sun in stages so as not to burn the leaves that have become used to shade. When fully hardened, plant out the new plants about 12 in apart.

Watering Lavender cotton is adapted to greatest rainfall from mid-autumn to mid-spring, with dry summers. Water to simulate these conditions. Once established, lavender cotton is tolerant of dry weather.

Fertilizing No fertilizing is needed.

Problems High summer rainfall and humidity can cause the plant to rot.

Pruning Shear the plant all over once or twice during the summer months and once again more heavily in autumn. This will keep the plant neat and very bushy.

THE SHARP, YELLOW FLOWERS of lavender cotton can upset a gray and silver scheme. If they upset you, trim them in spring.

HARVESTING

Picking Sprigs of leaves may be picked at any time as they are required.

Storage Tie sprigs of the leaves together and hang them upside down in a dark, airy place to dry. Then you can store the dried sprigs in an airtight container.

Freezing Not suitable for freezing.

USES

Craft Dried leaves can be used in potpourris and herbal sachets.

Gardening Lavender cotton is mostly used today as an edging plant along paths or drives or to border herb or vegetable gardens or other formal plantings. It can also be used as an unusual large-scale groundcover, especially if used on dry, sunny banks.

LEMON BALM
Melissa officinalis

FEATURES

A spreading perennial growing to 32 in high, lemon balm has small, serrated, nettle-like leaves with a lemon scent. They are supported on squarish stems with spikes of inconspicuous white flowers borne in the axils of the leaves during summer. These plants are very sensitive to frosts and may die back during winter, but established plants will regenerate in spring. Position lemon balm anywhere in the garden and especially near trees or plants that require bees to pollinate blossoms.

CONDITIONS

Climate   Balm comes from the hot regions of North Africa and southern Europe but is now cultivated successfully in warm zones and even some cooler areas. May be grown in the cooler months in the tropics.

Aspect   Prefers full sun or partial shade.

Soil   Soils should be rich in organic matter and kept moist and well mulched. Before planting, dig lime or dolomite into beds.

GROWING METHOD

Planting   Balm can be propagated three ways. Sow seeds directly into the garden in early to middle autumn or germinate them first in seed boxes and then transplant them during early spring. The germination period is long, and in the garden seedlings may need protection throughout winter. Mulching will help. Root division of the parent plant in early spring is also successful. Space the divided roots at least 24 in apart. Cuttings 4–5 in long can be taken from new spring growth. Cut below a node of the parent plant and remove the top leaves of the cuttings. Plant them deeply in small pots containing a 3:1 mix of river sand and peat moss and keep the soil moist.

Watering Fertilizing   Keep plants well watered in hot, dry spells. Apply complete plant food once in early spring when new growth begins.

ELIZABETHAN HOUSEWIVES used to rub furniture with sprigs of lemon balm to scent the wood. Bees love the tiny flowers.

Problems   Diseases most likely to strike are fungal. Brown leaves, or orange, powdery spots or pustules on the undersides of the leaves indicate rust infection. In moderately dry climates, powdery mildew may form a light gray powdery coating on leaves, flowers or young shoots, causing stunting or even defoliation of the plant. Treat both diseases with recommended fungal sprays. Spider mite is the most common insect pest. Spray with the appropriate insecticide.

Pruning   Keep straggly clumps in shape by pruning in spring. This promotes growth for summer.

HARVESTING

Picking   Pick fresh leaves as required. Whole stems may be cut when flowers begin to emerge and then dried. Leaves are most tender and full of flavor in spring.

Storage   Dry quickly by hanging cut stems in a cool, airy space. Rub dry leaves and flowers from the stems and store in airtight jars.

Freezing   Wrap in plastic wrap and freeze for 6 months.

USES

Culinary   Fresh leaves and flowers are used in salads and the leaves are also used in stuffings or sauces for poultry and fish. Lemon balm herbal teas are popular and fresh leaves can also be used to flavor cool summer drinks.

LEMON GRASS

Cymbopogon citratus

FEATURES

Lemon grass is a perennial grass of tropical regions. The narrow, ribbon-like, leafy stalks grow in clumps that reach about 3 ft or more in length. The leaves swell slightly at the base to form a fleshy stolon or underground stem. The stem is white and is also edible.

CONDITIONS

Climate
Native to the tropical regions of southeast Asia and Australia, lemon grass prefers to grow in warm or tropical regions but will grow in cooler areas if the frosts are not too severe and if the plant is heavily mulched in autumn to protect it throughout winter.

Aspect
Outside tropical areas lemon grass needs a protected, sunny position. In cooler climates, it can be grown in a container in a greenhouse or on a sunny, protected verandah—these conditions provide enough humidity to simulate its natural environment.

Soil
Lemon grass requires rich, fertile soils. Add plenty of organic matter in the form of compost, leaves, straw or decayed animal manures to the soil before planting and mulch constantly throughout the season to retain moisture levels.

GROWING METHOD

Planting
Lemon grass rarely flowers. Plant commercially purchased root stock or propagate in spring. To do this, divide the mature plant, breaking off portions from the outer edge of the clump, and then replant.

Watering
Water well as this plant requires a great deal of water, especially during the earlier stages of its growth.

Fertilizing
In spring and summer apply liquid or soluble fertilizer monthly.

Problems
Lemon grass is not attacked by any particular pests or diseases.

HARVESTING

Picking
Pick leaves or remove portions of the stem in summer as required.

Storage
Harvested portions will keep in the refrigerator for a few days. Lemon grass cannot be dried.

Freezing
Can be wrapped in plastic wrap and frozen for up to 6 months.

LEMON GRASS is an untidy grower but it can be kept presentable by trimming the foliage back in spring. The flowers are unexciting.

USES

Culinary
Lemon grass is common in the cuisines of southeast Asia. The "sweet-sour," lemony flavor of the leaves is used in herbal teas, or pieces can be tied together and used to flavor marinades and in cooking. The white, fleshy stem is chopped and used to flavor cooked dishes such as curries, fish or soups. It may be discarded after cooking. It can also be incorporated into fresh salads.

LEMON VERBENA
Aloysia triphylla

FEATURES

A large, bushy, deciduous shrub that can grow to over 6 ft in height, lemon verbena has long, lemony-scented, narrow leaves. Spikes or sprays of small white to mauve flowers appear in the axils of the leaves in summer. The leaves give this plant its herby quality, and fragrance can be released simply by brushing against them in the garden. It can be grown in containers and in cooler climates indoors, although container plants do not reach the same height as specimens grown in the garden.

CONDITIONS

Climate   Prefers moist, warm climates. High summer humidity in the tropics may cause it to be short lived. Sensitive to cold weather and best grown in containers in cooler regions.

Aspect   Prefers a sheltered, sunny position with protection in winter.

Soil   Likes rich soils. Needs mulching to protect against frosts.

GROWING METHOD

Planting   Grow from softwood cuttings in summer or hardwood cuttings in autumn. Trim a 5 in piece from the parent bush, removing a third of the upper leaves and a few of the lower leaves. Place in a mix of two-thirds coarse sand and one-third peat moss. Moisten the soil and cover the pot with a plastic bag to create a mini greenhouse. Pot in good quality potting mix when the cutting has taken root and shows renewed leaf growth. Replant in the garden when the plant is growing strongly.

Watering   The plant is reasonably tolerant of dry conditions and normal garden watering is sufficient for growth.

Fertilizing   Use complete plant food every six weeks or apply controlled release granules as directed on the packet.

Problems   Spider mite and whitefly weaken the plant by sucking plant juices from the leaves and stems. Hose leaves frequently or use organic soap and pyrethrum or recommended chemical sprays for these pests. Watch out for powdery mildew, which causes foliage to wilt, on the upper surfaces of the leaves. Spray or remove diseased plants.

Pruning   Prune each season to contain its straggly growth habit. This is an ideal plant to train into a formal shape as a standard or topiary.

THIS HERB was introduced to European gardens from Chile in 1746. The name Aloysia *honours Queen Maria Louisa of Spain.*

HARVESTING

Picking   Sprigs of leaves can be harvested all year long. If leaves are required for drying, cut the bush back during summer and early winter. Hang the branches in a cool, airy place and strip off the leaves when they are dry.

Storage   Store dried leaves in airtight jars. Fragrance remains for some years.

Freezing   Wrap in plastic wrap and then freeze for up to 6 months.

USES

Culinary   Dried leaves can be used for herbal tea or in cooking where a lemony flavor is required, as with fish, poultry, marinades, salad dressings and puddings.

Craft   The strong fragrance makes dried leaves a popular component of herb potpourris and sachet fillings.

Gardening   Lemon verbena is an attractive border plant.

LOVAGE
Levisticum officinale

FEATURES

A very tall perennial herb that reaches 3–6 ft, this plant looks quite spectacular when growing in the garden. Dark green to yellowish leaves become smaller towards the top of the plant and break into wedge-shaped, ridged leaflets. Greenish flowers appear in summer, and then are followed by ¼ in long, light brown, grooved, aromatic seeds. The hollow, ribbed stems of lovage look and taste like celery and there is a longish tap root that is much like a carrot. Lovage may die back to ground level over winter but it will regenerate in the following spring.

CONDITIONS

Climate   Lovage is not suitable for hot tropical areas. It grows well in cool climates, tolerating extremes of frost.

Aspect   Prefers full sun or semi-shade.

Soil   Moist, fertile, well-drained alkaline soil provides optimum growing conditions for lovage. Dig plenty of compost and decayed animal manure deep into the soil and if acidity is a problem, add some lime or dolomite into the top soil. In warmer areas, mulch the soil around each plant to keep it cool, moist and free of weeds.

GROWING METHOD

Planting   Sow seeds in late summer through autumn directly into the garden, or plant seedlings approximately 12 in apart. Mature plants that have been in the garden for at least two seasons can be propagated by dividing the roots in autumn or spring.

Watering   Water well so that the soil is moist, especially in hot, dry weather.

Fertilising   Give an application of complete plant food once in early spring.

Problems   Aphids love lovage and can transmit viral diseases to the plant. Hose vigorously to break their cycle or treat with organic or recommended insecticidal sprays. Leaf miner maggots will tunnel into leaves causing white blotches. Remove infected leaves.

Pruning   Prune flowers in summer for a bushier plant.

LOVAGE has been long grown and used in cooking: the ancient Roman writer Apicius featured its mild flavor in many of his recipes.

HARVESTING

Picking   Harvest any part of the plant as needed. Do not cut the central stem when picking the leaves.

Storage   Stems, leaves and seeds can be dried and kept in airtight jars.

Freezing   Leaves can be blanched in boiling water and then quick frozen wrapped in small lots or frozen within ice cubes. Can be frozen for up to 6 months.

USES

Culinary   Leaves, stems and seeds are substitutes for celery. Try leaves and stems in fresh salads and dried seeds in soups, casseroles, sauces and pickling mixtures, or savory biscuits. Lovage is also used in teas, vinegars and butters.

MARJORAM
Origanum majorana, syn. *Majorana hortensis*

FEATURES

This variety of marjoram, known as sweet or knotted marjoram, is the one most commonly grown in herb gardens. A tender, bushy perennial herb, it is usually grown as an annual as it does not survive cold winters. Grows to 2 ft or more, producing small, oval leaves covered with fine hair. The leaves are light green on top and gray-green underneath and are borne on short stalks. During summer very small, white to lilac flowers appear in clusters, first in knot-like shapes, and produce tiny, light brown seeds.

CONDITIONS

Climate   Grows in warm zones; must be well drained in areas of summer rain. Doesn't like frost but does well in containers indoors in cooler areas. In the tropics grow as a cool-season annual.

Aspect   Prefers full sun.

Soil   Does best in quite rich soils containing plenty of compost and decayed animal manure. Add lime or dolomite if the soil is too acidic. Shallow cultivate to keep soil free of weeds.

GROWING METHOD

Planting   Seeds are slow to germinate and are usually planted in seed trays. Pot in small containers after the first few true leaves have formed, and then put into the garden in spring when the seedlings are established. Plant in small clumps 6 in apart. Propagation by cuttings is also possible, during autumn. Take a 2 in piece of woody stem from the parent plant, trim the leaves from the cutting and root it in a mixture of two-thirds coarse sand to one-third peat moss. Transplant in spring when the root structure is established and new growth appears on the stem. Roots of a mature plant can also be divided in autumn.

Watering   Water adequately but do not overwater.

Fertilizing   Little additional fertilizer is needed in well-mulched soil. Apply liquid organic fertilizer or seaweed-based conditioner every six weeks.

Problems   Damping off of seedlings is one problem of this herb: they become water-soaked, shrivel and die. Keep seed beds warm and use good quality, sterile seed mix. Bad drainage will bring on this disease, and root rot in older plants. Pests include aphids and spider mite. Hose down, or treat with insecticide.

THIS FAVORITE HERB of Italian cookery was regarded by the Romans as sacred to Venus: they wore marjoram at their weddings.

Pruning   Flowers can be pruned at knot stage to maintain the shape of the bush.

HARVESTING

Picking   Pick leaves for culinary use at any time. Harvest leaves to be dried and unopened knot-like flowers in summer—the stems can be cut down to 2 in above the ground—and hang them to dry in a cool, shady spot.

Storage   Remove leaves and buds from stems and store in airtight jars. Discard stems.

Freezing   Chop finely, mix with a little water and freeze in ice cubes.

USES

Culinary   The taste resembles that of a mild oregano and can be substituted for it. It is often used in the French bouquet garni. Fresh leaves and flowers can be used in salads, stuffings for meat and poultry, or in marinades. The flavor blends with most vegetable dishes and can also be used to flavor vinegars and oils. Dried, it makes a refreshing herbal tea.

Craft   Marjoram adds fragrance in potpourris.

MINT
Mentha

MINT IS VERY INVASIVE, spreading rapidly by underground runners. If you cannot afford the space to give it its head, as here, it can be grown in a tub as long as you remember to keep it well watered. The prettily variegated apple mint is less rampageous than the green-leaved kinds.

FEATURES

There are many varieties of mint, but all are perennials and they all have square stems and invasive, spreading roots. They can be prostrate or upright in nature. The simple, light to dark green or mottled leaves have toothed edges and their own individual fragrance, depending on variety. The small, flowers are purple, pink or white and come in whorls on terminal spikes. They appear in summer. Because of their invasive nature, mints are best grown in containers or in garden beds that have a solid border at least 20 in deep.

CONDITIONS

Climate   Grows in most climates as it is indigenous to many countries and continents. Mint will even grow in arid areas if it is provided with a regular supply of water.

Aspect   Mint prefers a semi-shaded position and can be grown indoors in a container. It will grow in full sun if the soil is kept moist.

Soil   Soil should be moderately rich and well mulched so that it retains moisture. The addition of too much organic matter or fresh manures to the bed will, however, encourage rust diseases.

GROWING METHOD

Planting   Most mints can be raised from seed (although some varieties, such as spearmint, cannot be propagated this way), but root division during spring and summer is the easiest method of propagation. Lift runners, divide them and replant in rich, moist soil.

Watering   Keep soil moist as mint must always have plenty of water.

Fertilizing   No fertilizer is necessary if planted in well-mulched soil.

ABOVE: The tiny Corsican mint is the most strongly scented and flavored of all mints. It makes a delightful groundcover.

TOP LEFT: Spearmint is the most widely used type of mint and the one you will be offered at a nursery if you ask for "mint."

BOTTOM LEFT: Eau-de-cologne mint is rather bitter and must be used sparingly in cooking. It lends its scent to eau de cologne.

Problems   Mint flea beetle is a tiny, dark, oval pest that is continually on the move when disturbed. It eats holes in the leaves and its larvae will eat into the roots of the plant. To treat it, keep weeds down and spread lime around the bush. Spider mite can be treated with an appropriate spray. Discoloring of leaves may indicate mint rust, which can be treated with sulphur dustings, or a form of wilt that causes leaves to brown and drop. Treat wilt by removing diseased plants and do not feed with high nitrogen fertilizers.

Pruning   Frequent pruning of the stems forces lateral branching and healthier plants.

HARVESTING

Picking   Young, fresh leaves can be picked at any time. The younger the leaf, the tenderer and tastier it will be.

Storage   Leaves can be dried by placing them on a rack in a cool, airy space. When they are dry, crumble them and store in airtight jars.

Freezing   Fresh leaves can be chopped and frozen in small packages or in ice cubes.

USES

Culinary   Mints have a wide range of flavors from the fruity taste of apple mint to the perfume-like one of the eau-de-cologne variety, making them very useful, especially in sauces or jellies. They can be used fresh in salads, drinks, vinegars or as a garnish to vegetables, often turning a bland taste into an exciting experience. Dried mints can be used in place of some of the salt in soups.

Gardening   Some organic gardeners promote the growth of mint around apple trees to ward off moths, but there is some doubt about its effectiveness.

NASTURTIUM
Tropaeolum majus

FEATURES

A trailing perennial that can be trained so as to reach up to 6 ft, nasturtium is nevertheless usually grown as an annual, especially in colder areas and in the tropics. The wide leaves are roundish and dark green to variegated in color and have a peppery taste. The funnel-shaped, five-petaled and spurred flowers appear in late spring and summer and range from creamy white through yellow to salmon, brilliant orange and red. Some varieties have double flowers and all have a slight perfume. The edible buds each produce one seed. This plant grows well in containers.

CONDITIONS

Climate Native to South America and now cultivated in most climates. Grow as a cool season annual in colder areas and the tropics.

Aspect Prefers full sun although dwarf varieties will grow in semi-shade. Leaf growth is more pronounced in shady situations.

Soil Nasturtiums do not like an over-rich soil but good drainage is necessary.

GROWING METHOD

Planting Sow seeds from midsummer through to spring in hot and tropical climates, from spring through to summer in warm zones and during spring in colder areas. Sow several seeds of the trailing varieties together in clumps set about 32 in apart. Plant dwarf varieties 16 in apart. Sow the seeds 1 in deep directly into the garden bed or containers where they are to grow and keep the soil just moist.

Watering Do not water excessively, especially when plants are well established.

Fertilizing More flowers and seeds will be produced if you hold back on the fertilizer and compost. Fertilizing encourages the growth of leaves.

Problems Sap-sucking aphids love nasturtiums. Vigorously hose the pest off or treat the plant with an appropriate spray. Bacterial wilt and leaf spot are common diseases. Don't cultivate while plants are wet and remove all diseased plants from the garden.

TROPAEOLUM means "a little trophy," so named because the shield-shaped leaves and golden, helmet-like flowers suggested piles of armor.

HARVESTING

Picking Pick any part of the plant as required.

Storage Leaves and flowers do not store well and should be used immediately. Buds and seeds can be pickled in vinegar, stored in airtight jars and used at a later date.

Freezing Wrap in plastic wrap; freeze up to 6 months.

USES

Culinary All parts of this herb are edible. Fresh leaves and flowers are used in salads or the flowers can be used alone as a garnish. Buds and seeds are used as a substitute for capers.

Gardening Because they are so attractive to aphids, nasturtiums are an excellent companion plant for vegetables such as cabbages, broccoli and other brassica. The aphids will flock to the nasturtium and leave the vegetables alone.

OREGANO
Origanum vulgare

FEATURES

Oregano is very closely related to marjoram and is often confused with it. Three varieties of this summer flowering perennial are widely grown. Common or wild oregano, *O. vulgare*, is a small shrub growing to 12 in high, with woody stems and oval, soft, hairy leaves and tiny, white flowers. Golden oregano, *O. vulgare* 'Aureum,' is very decorative in the garden but will tend to spread if uncontrolled. The leaves are golden-yellow in color and the flowers are pink. Greek or white oregano, *O. vulgare* 'Viride,' is taller than the other varieties, reaching 20 in. Its leaves are dark green, covered with a white, hairy bloom and have a very pungent flavor. The flowers are white.

CONDITIONS

Climate   Prefers warm, relatively dry climates where most rain falls in winter. In areas of summer rain soil must be very well drained. In the tropics grow it as a cool season annual. It does not like frost but grows satisfactorily in cooler regions as a container herb.

Aspect   Needs full sun or partial shade.

Soil   Likes well-drained, not too rich garden soil. Mulch to keep soils moist in hot, dry weather.

GROWING METHOD

Planting   Sow seeds in spring, in damp, warm, seed-raising mix. Temperatures need to be above 68°F for the best results. Transplant seedlings into the garden when well established. More often, propagate by root division in late spring as it spreads by underground stems, or propagate by layering. Scarify the under surface of the branch, peg it down and cover with soil. Keep damp until roots form, cut it off and replant. Replace plants every couple of years as the stems become woody.

Watering   Keep plants well watered and do not let the soil dry out.

Fertilizing   Apply liquid organic fertilizer or seaweed-based soil conditioner every six weeks.

Problems   Aphids, leaf miner and spider mite should be treated with appropriate insecticidal sprays. Hosing leaves may bring temporary relief but if infestations are bad, remove and burn diseased plants. Plants affected by root rot, which is caused by bad drainage, should be removed; rotate plants every three years.

GOLDEN-LEAVED OREGANO is more decorative than the ordinary green version and just as fine in flavor and scent.

Pruning   Prune after flowering to keep plant compact.

HARVESTING

Picking   Pick fresh leaves throughout the growing season as required. Cut whole stems before flowering and hang them up to dry in a cool, shady spot.

Storage   Strip dry leaves from stems and store in airtight jars.

Freezing   Wrap in plastic wrap; freeze up to 6 months.

USES

Culinary   Oregano is widely used as a flavoring, especially in Mediterranean-style cooking, in sauces, soups and casseroles, as well as in vinegars and butters.

Gardening   Plants make excellent groundcovers.

ORRIS ROOT

Iris x *germanica* var. *florentina*

FEATURES

Orris root is a rhizomatous perennial iris. It consists of a fan-shaped clump of stiff, upright, sword-shaped leaves in gray-green with distinct parallel veins. The showy flowers appear in spring or summer and are white flushed with mauve or soft lilac-blue. The plant grows to a height of approximately 16 in. Once dried, the root exudes a strong aroma reminiscent of violets, a property not shared with other irises.

CONDITIONS

Climate   Best suited to cool climates. Can be grown in warm areas if they are not excessively hot, wet and humid in summer.

Aspect   Full sun is essential.

Soil   Plants do best in well-drained, slightly alkaline soil to which a proportion of rotted organic matter has been added. Take care not to over-enrich the soil with either manures or fertilizers as these plants do not grow well with high levels of nitrogen.

GROWING METHOD

Planting   Grow from divisions of the rhizome taken after bloom. The plant is lifted and its creeping rhizome cut into sections. Each section should have its own fan of leaves and a growing point. The old center of the clump, which has flowered, will never do so again and should be discarded. Cut the leaves in half crosswise, and then replant the rhizomes about 14 in apart into soil that has been well dug over. Lay them horizontally so that about half the rhizome is above ground level—deeper planting will cause the rhizomes to rot.

Watering   Keep soil evenly moist during the warmer months. Orris root is not particularly tolerant of prolonged dry conditions.

Fertilizing   Dig in a lean ration of complete plant food at planting time, but no other feeding will be necessary. A thin mulch of very old, rotted manure or compost may be applied around the base of the plant.

Problems   No particular problems.

ORRIS ROOT has been cultivated in the fields around the Italian city of Florence for centuries. "Orris" is an old English version of "iris."

HARVESTING

Picking   Dig out the root in early summer. A few pieces of young rhizome can be replanted to provide future crops and the rest can then be put aside for processing.

Storage   Clean the root and cut it into small segments. Dry it in the sun and then store it in an airtight jar in the fridge. The fragrance of the root does not develop fully until about a year has passed.

Freezing   Not suitable for freezing.

USES

Craft   Orris root is mainly used to impart a heady violet scent to potpourris. It also acts as a preservative in such dried material. Do take care, however, as orris root may cause sneezing, coughing and other allergic reactions in some sensitive people.

PARSLEY
Petroselinum

NO NEED TO DESPAIR *when parsley flowers as the flowers are* *edible. This Italian parsley can also be used in flower arrangements.*

HERE GROWING *with lettuces, sage and nasturtiums, curly parsley* *makes a very attractive addition to any bed of herbs and vegetables.*

CURLY PARSLEY *is the prettiest of garnishes and the essential* *ingredient in a bouquet garni. Here it grows with white alyssum.*

FEATURES

Parsley grows from a strong tap root with erect, 12 in tall stems bearing divided, feather-like, small leaves which may be flattish or curly depending on variety. Tiny, yellowish-green flowers arranged in clusters are borne on tall stalks in summer, and produce small, brown, oval and ribbed seeds. Common varieties of this biennial or short-lived perennial plant include curly parsley, *P. crispum*, plain-leaved or Italian parsley, *P. crispum* var. *neapolitanum*, and Hamburg or turnip-rooted parsley, *P. crispum* var. *tuberosum*.

CONDITIONS

Climate   Parsley likes a warm to coolish climate. Grow these plants as a cool season annual in the tropics or in a container in areas where there are frosts.

Aspect   Prefers full sun or possibly part shade.

Soil   Parsley plants need only a moderately rich, well-drained soil.

GROWING METHOD

Planting   Grow from seed planted during the warmer months when the soil is warm, above 50°F. Germination takes 6–8 weeks, and seeds are usually brought on in seed trays before they are planted out. Before planting, create optimum conditions by soaking the seeds in warm water for 24 hours and pouring boiling water over the soil to raise the temperature. Transplant the seedlings out, 10 in apart, after they have grown several true leaves. If grown in a container, the pots should be at least 8 in deep, and the longer tap root of Hamburg parsley will require an even deeper one. Once plants are established in the garden, the mature plants can be left to self-sow when they go to seed in summer months in their second year of growth.

ITS FINE TEXTURE AND RICH GREEN COLOR make parsley an ideal edging plant. Here it is used to set off the varied tones and textures of a formal vegetable garden, but it would look equally fine as a foil for brightly colored flowers.

Watering	Keep soil moist and do not let it dry out in dry weather.
Fertilizing	Side feedings of a nitrogen-rich liquid fertilizer will promote more leaf growth on these plants.
Problems	Parsley worm, root-knot nematode and carrot weevils, which devour the foliage, stunt the growth and burrow into the top and root, are the main pests. Practice crop rotation and destroy affected plants. Watch for white fungal growth near the base of the plant and a brownish crust on the soil, indicative of crown rot. Treat as for pests.
Pruning	Parsley can be kept productive by frequent pruning and by nipping out the seed stalks whenever they appear.

HARVESTING

Picking	New growth comes from the center of the stem, and so always pick parsley from the outside of the plant. Pick this vitamin-rich, nutritious herb as needed.
Storage	Broad-leaved Italian parsley, with its stronger taste, gives a better result when dried than the other varieties.
Freezing	Curly parsley freezes well. Wrap it first in plastic wrap and put it in the freezer for up to 6 months.

USES

Culinary	Parsley is used in salads, as a garnish and in cooking. Hamburg parsley is used like a root vegetable. Fresh parsley is a breath freshener.

PURSLANE

Portulaca oleracea

FEATURES

This spreading, succulent annual is very adaptable, growing as a weed in many parts of the world. Purslane forms a mat-like growth, which makes it a useful groundcover in areas where it will not spread unduly. It has bright, light green, spoon-shaped leaves on trailing, fleshy stems that are reddish in color. The small, bright yellow flowers are produced at stem junctions during the spring and summer months. They will open only when the plants are in sunlight.

CONDITIONS

Climate   Purslane can be grown almost everywhere, from cool zones to tropical climates, as it has a wide range of tolerance.

Aspect   Full sun is preferable but plants will tolerate shade for part of the day.

Soil   Purslane is not fussy about soil so long as it drains freely, but plants will produce succulent leaves more quickly if they are grown in fertile, sandy soil that contains some rotted organic matter.

GROWING METHOD

Planting   Sow the seeds directly where they are to grow in early spring or, in cooler areas, after all danger of frost has passed. In tropical areas, sow them during the autumn months. Purslane can also be started from cuttings that are taken anytime from mid-spring onwards. Make the cuttings about 2 in long, strip off the lower leaves and insert the cuttings into small containers of very sandy potting mix or seed-raising mix. Keep the containers warm and moist, and put them in a bright but not sunny spot until the roots have formed. The plants can then be planted out in the garden in their permanent positions.

Watering   Having water-storing leaves and stems, purslane is well able to cope with dryness, but for the best quality leaves keep the soil evenly moist during spring and summer.

Fertilizing   Fertilizing will not be necessary if purslane is grown in fertile soil. Elsewhere, water the plants once a month with a high nitrogen soluble fertilizer.

Problems   No pest or disease problems but flowers should be routinely removed to minimize unwanted spread by seed.

PICK ONLY THE TENDEREST YOUNG LEAVES, preferably before plants flower. Old leaves are apt to be tough and tasteless.

HARVESTING

Picking   Let the plants grow until they are about 4 in across and then pick the stems and leaves as they are needed. Plants regrow quickly.

Storage   Cut purslane stems may be stored in the refrigerator for a few days.

Freezing   Not suitable for freezing.

USES

Culinary   Leaves and stems contain large amounts of iron and have a fresh, acid taste. They may be eaten raw in salads, or they can be lightly stir-fried or steamed as a vegetable.

ROCKET

Eruca vesicaria subspecies *sativa*

FEATURES

Rocket is an annual with long, deeply lobed, dark green leaves, often tinted red, and simple, cross-shaped, creamy-white flowers. Leaves have a pleasant, peppery, nutty flavor and are produced in a dense rosette at the base of the plant, from which rise the branching stems. The stems, which may reach 3 ft, bear flowers, followed by plump seed heads which shatter when dry, each dispersing hundreds of seeds. Rocket grows very fast and several crops may be raised during spring and summer.

CONDITIONS

Climate
Best suited to cool and warm climates but grows reasonably well in the tropical winter.

Aspect
During spring grow in full sun but in summer and in the tropics, a cooler, partly shaded spot helps slow the plant's rush to seed and thus lengthens its useful life.

Soil
Grow in fertile, well-drained soil enriched with rotted manure or compost. Rocket will grow in poor soils, too, but its leaves will be tough and more bitter.

GROWING METHOD

Planting
Sow seeds in early spring ¾ in deep and 14 in apart. If sharp frosts are still likely then, sow indoors in trays of seed-raising mix placed in a sunny window. Plant out when the seedlings are big enough to handle and frosts are light or have passed. As rocket grows fast and young leaves are the most palatable, new sowings should be made approximately every four weeks. When the latest batch of seedlings is big enough to pick from, pull out the previous batch. You can continue sowing rocket until about mid-autumn. In the tropics, start sowing in late autumn and continue until the end of winter.

Watering
For fastest growth and sweetest, best tasting leaves, keep the plants well watered. Plants enjoy consistent moisture but not wetness around their roots, and so make sure that the soil drains well.

Fertilizing
Dig in a ration of complete plant food at sowing time and then water the plants over every two weeks or so with a soluble, high nitrogen fertilizer.

ROCKET was loved by the Romans and remains a favorite salad herb in Italy. It is a native of the Mediterranean.

Problems
Snails and slugs may damage the leaves of freshly sown plants in early spring and autumn. Either pick them off by hand or lay snail bait. As rocket can quickly become an invasive weed it is important to prevent flowering except to provide seeds for resowing. On most plants, snap off flower stems as they rise or, better still, replace flowering plants with new, young plants.

HARVESTING

Picking
Start picking young leaves about five weeks after seedlings have emerged, sooner in summer when growth is faster. Seeds are harvested when the pods have plumped out and are beginning to look dry.

Storage
Seeds may be stored in airtight jars but leaves must be used fresh.

Freezing
Not suitable for freezing.

USES

Culinary
Young leaves give green salads an appealing piquancy or add them late to stir fries. Ripe seed pods are also edible.

Medicinal
Rocket is said to be a stimulant and good for warding off colds.

ROSEMARY
Rosmarinus officinalis

THIS STANDARD ROSEMARY grows in a pot with Mexican daisies providing a dash of color around its base.

TRADITIONALLY a bringer of good fortune, rosemary is often grown by a path or steps, where its fragrance can also be enjoyed as you pass.

FEATURES

A perennial, evergreen, woody shrub, rosemary has thin, needle-like leaves, glossy green above and whitish to gray-green and hairy below. They have a fragrance reminiscent of pine needles. In spring, small-lobed flowers appear among the leaves. They are pale blue to pinkish, depending on the variety. There are several varieties of rosemary, ranging in habit from the upright (*R. officinalis*) to the dwarf (*R. officinalis* 'Nana') and the prostrate (*R. officinalis* 'Prostratus'). Other popular varieties are Blue Lagoon rosemary (*R. officinalis* 'Collingwood Ingram') and pink rosemary (*R. officinalis* 'Rosea'). Rosemary bushes can be between 20 in and 6 ft high, depending on variety. This is a good herb to grow in containers, and it also grows well in seaside positions where not much else will grow, as it will withstand salt and wind.

CONDITIONS

Climate   Grows well in warm, relatively dry climates with most rain in winter. It can withstand the dry, windy conditions along coastal plains. Tolerates cooler climates—is best grown there in containers.

Aspect   Likes full sun and a reasonably dry position.
Soil   Needs well-drained soil to lessen the risk of root rot, and is more fragrant in alkaline soils. If acidity is a problem, dig in 8 oz per square yard of lime or dolomite before planting.

GROWING METHOD

Planting   Propagate mainly from cuttings and layering. Seeds are not often used because they have long germination times and tend not to come true to type. Take 4 in long cuttings in late spring (and early autumn in warmer climates), trim off the upper and lower leaves and place the cuttings in small pots containing a moist mixture of two-thirds coarse sand and one-third peat moss. Cover with a plastic dome and set aside in a semi-shaded position until roots and new leaves form. Or scarify the underside of a lower branch and firmly secure it to the soil with a wire peg. Cover with sand and keep moist until roots form. Cut off and replant.

Watering   Prefers soil to be on the drier side; give average garden watering.

Fertilizing   Fertilizer is not needed.

ROSEMARY BUSHES will take hard pruning but don't cut into leafless wood, which will not sprout. That's what has happened here.

ROSEMARY FLOWERS have a subtle scent, sweeter than the leaves. They are a clear blue (photos give them this pinkish tinge).

Problems Look out for mealy bug, scale, spider mite and whitefly. Treat with appropriate insecticidal sprays. Botrytis blight, a fungal growth affecting all parts of plant, and root rot can be treated by improving drainage and removing yellowing leaves and dead flowers or badly infected plants. Frequent summer rainfall can cause the shrub to rot.

Pruning Prune if compact bushes are desired. 'Blue Lagoon' has a very straggly growing habit.

HARVESTING

Picking Fresh leaves or sprigs 2–4 in long can be picked as required. Pick flowers in spring.

Storage Dry sprigs in a cool, dry place, strip leaves from the stems and store in airtight jars.

Freezing Store sprigs in plastic bags and freeze for up to 6 months. To use, crumble before thawing.

USES

Cosmetic Rosemary rinses help control greasy hair.

Culinary Fresh, dried or frozen leaves are used in cooking, marinades and salad dressings. Leaves are used in vinegars, oils, teas and butters. Fresh flowers are good in salads or as decorations for puddings and desserts.

Craft It is used in potpourris and herb wreaths.

'SEVEN SEAS' has the richest blue flowers of any rosemary cultivar. Its growth is upright, but less dense and compact than most rosemaries.

RUE

Ruta graveolens

FEATURES

Rue is a rounded, shrubby perennial with many stems rising from a woody base. It can grow to about 3 ft tall with a similar spread. Leaves are strongly aromatic but the color varies and may be green, blue-green or variegated. Foliage is finely divided and makes an attractive backgound for the small, spicily fragrant, yellowish flowers which appear in late spring or summer.

CONDITIONS

Climate Grows in cool or warm climates, especially well in areas where most rain falls in winter. Dislikes summer humidity.

Aspect In cooler areas where summers are mild, full sun is essential. In warmer areas rue will tolerate some but not full shade.

Soil Deep, well-drained but rather poor, sandy or gravelly soil suits rue. In its native range it grows in dry, rocky places on limestone soils. Over-rich soils lead to lax, rampant growth and loss of compactness.

GROWING METHOD

Planting Sow seeds in spring in trays of seed-raising mix. Keep moist and place in bright, dappled shade until germination is complete. Gradually expose to greater amounts of sun before planting into the final position. Alternatively, new plants can be grown from cuttings taken towards the end of summer. Select growth that has matured but is not yet woody and place 4 in cuttings into pots of very sandy potting mix. Keep the mix moist and place pots in bright shade until roots have formed. Where stems of mature plants touch the ground, they will often form roots. These rooted "layers" can be detached from the parent plant, dug up and relocated.

Watering Water deeply each fortnight from mid-autumn to mid-spring as this simulates the plant's natural conditions. Water in summer only in dry areas and only if the plant looks as if it needs water.

Fertilizing No fertilizing is needed.

Problems Usually no pest and disease problems but high summer heat, rain and humidity can lead to fungus diseases of the leaves and root rot. The plant's sap can severely irritate sensitive skins. Wear gloves whenever the plant is handled and do not let it touch hands, face or body.

MEDIEVAL MONKS believed rue encouraged chastity and grew it in their gardens, calling it "herb of grace." They also used it to kill fleas.

Pruning Untidy plants may be pruned hard in early spring. Using sharp shears, cut back to a main framework of branches. New growth will restore the plant's rounded, bushy habit. Less untidy plants may be made more compact by a light, all-over shearing in mid-spring.

HARVESTING

Picking Rue has toxic properties and must be used with extreme caution. Leaves may be picked at any time to make an insecticidal infusion.

Storage Leafy stems may be bunched and dried in a dark, airy place for later use.

Freezing Not suitable for freezing.

USES

Gardening Rue is a decorative plant that infuses the garden with its herbal aroma, especially on hot days. It is a good companion for other Mediterranean plants such as lavender and echium. An insect repellent for use on ornamental or productive plants can be made from the leaves.

SAGE
Salvia

PURPLE SAGE grows here in this wonderfully exuberant herb and vegetable garden, contributing to the subtle harmony of colors. It has lavender cotton growing on its left and a fancy-leaved lettuce on its right.

FEATURES

Sage is a small, woody, perennial shrub growing to about 30 in. The long, oval, gray-green leaves, velvety in texture, have a slightly bitter, camphor-like taste, while the flowers, borne on spikes in spring, are colored from pink to red, purple, blue or white, depending on variety. There are many varieties of this beautiful and hardy herb. The most common edible types are common or garden sage (*S. officinalis*), purple sage (*S.* x *superba*), pineapple sage (*S. elegans*, syn. *S. rutilans*) and golden or variegated sage (*S. officinalis* 'Variegata'). Other sages are grown purely for their decorative qualities in the garden, chief among them being clary sage (*S. sclarea*). Sage needs to be replaced every four years or so as the plant becomes woody.

CONDITIONS

Climate   Tolerate most climates with the exception of the tropics. In areas of extreme heat or cold, the plants are best grown in containers.

Aspect   Prefers a sunny, sheltered position.
Soil   Garden beds in which sage is to be grown should have a rich, non-clayish soil. Prepare the beds by digging in 8 oz of lime or dolomite, followed by plenty of organic matter such as compost and decayed animal manure. Good drainage is absolutely essential for sage plants, and so you may find it necessary to raise the beds to at least 8 in above the surrounding garden level.

GROWING METHOD

Planting   Plant seeds in late spring in seed-raising boxes, and when seedlings are 3–4 in tall plant them out into the garden, spacing them 18 in apart. Cuttings, 4 in long, can be taken in late autumn or spring. Remove the upper and lower leaves, and plant the cuttings in small pots containing a soil mix of two-thirds coarse sand and one-third peat moss. Water and then cover pots with a plastic bag to create a mini-greenhouse. Plant out when the cutting has developed roots and new leaves. Sage may also be layered—scarify the lower side of a branch and peg it into the soil to take root.

SALVIA GRAHAMII, *very strong in flavor, is a yard-tall shrub from Mexico, usually grown for its long display of bright flowers.*

THE PURPLE-BLUE FLOWERS *of common sage go very well with its gray leaves. Trim them off when they fade to keep the garden neat.*

THE LEAVES *of purple sage fade as they mature, but new shoots continue to add touches of color all summer. Flowers are purple-blue.*

Watering	Give a deep soaking once a week.
Fertilizing	Apply complete plant food at planting time. Give an application once each spring.
Problems	Slugs can be a problem. Pick them off by hand or set a stale beer trap in a saucer with the rim just at soil level. Spider mites will need to be sprayed with an insecticide. If the plant suddenly flops over for no apparent reason this is probably due to bacterial wilt affecting the vascular system. Remove affected plants before the disease spreads. Avoid root rot by providing good drainage.
Pruning	Prune off flowers to stop the plant from setting seed.

HARVESTING

Picking	Leaves or flowers can be picked at any time as required. For drying purposes, harvest leaves before flowering begins.
Storage	Dry leaves on racks in a cool, airy place and then store them in airtight jars.
Freezing	Leaves can be chopped, packed in plastic wrap and then frozen for up to 6 months.

USES

Cosmetic	Sage hair rinses, used regularly, will darken gray hair.
Culinary	Fresh or dried leaves are used extensively as a flavoring in stuffings, marinades and cooking. The individual fruity flavor of pineapple sage complements citrus fruits and the edible flowers look decorative in salads or as a garnish. Sage leaves of many varieties can also be used in herbal teas, in vinegars and in various herb butters.

SALAD BURNET
Sanguisorba minor

THE GRAYISH LEAVES OF SALAD BURNET make a pretty, fragrant groundcover. In the old days, doctors used them like cotton wool to absorb the blood from wounds, hence the botanical name Sanguisorba *which is derived from the Latin words for "blood" and "to suck."*

FEATURES

This small but bushy perennial herb grows in a clump about 20 in high. The roundish, gray-green, toothed leaves are borne on a central stem which droops down close to the ground. Flower stems, growing to about 24 in high, appear in summer and produce pinkish-red, oval flowers. Burnet is an attractive border plant and it can be grown successfully in pots.

CONDITIONS

Climate Warm to cold regions are best. Burnet is not suited to the tropics.
Aspect Likes a sunny, well-drained position.
Soil Most soil types are suitable. Add lime or dolomite if the soil conditions are acidic. Ensure soil is well drained at all times.

GROWING METHOD

Planting Salad burnet readily self-sows. Germinate seed in seed-raising boxes, cover the seed lightly with mix and keep the soil damp. When the seedlings are 2–4 in tall, plant them into the garden or containers, spaced 12–16 in apart. Propagation by division of the parent plant during autumn or spring is also possible.
Watering Water thoroughly in hot weather but do not overwater in winter as the plant tolerates much drier conditions then.

Fertilizing Apply complete plant food once each year in early spring and water in well.
Problems Burnet suffers from root rot if the soil is not well drained. If conditions are too damp in winter crown rot will develop and the plants will turn yellow and die.
Pruning Removal of flower stalks will stimulate new leaf growth.

HARVESTING

Picking Pick the leaves when they are still quite young and tender.
Storage Cannot be successfully stored.
Freezing Cannot be frozen.

USES

Culinary Use burnet only when fresh. Leaves have a cucumber scent and flavor and are much prized in salads or with fresh vegetables. They can also be chopped and included in cooked soups or sauces. Freshly picked sprigs look effective as a garnish in summer drinks.
Gardening As a companion plant, burnet does very well if grown close by beds of thyme and mint.

SAVORY

Satureja

BOTH SAVORIES, winter and summer, are alike in their four-petaled, white flowers. This is the perennial winter savory.

SUMMER SAVORY, being an annual, has to be sown afresh each spring. Many cooks consider it superior in flavor to winter savory.

FEATURES

Summer savory (*S. hortensis*) is an annual plant growing to about 20 in and with small, narrow, grayish leaves that turn slightly purple during summer and early autumn. The leaves are attached directly to a pinkish stem, and small white flowers appear on the plant in summer. The winter savories, both the upright (*S. montana*) and the prostrate (*S. montana* 'Repens') varieties, are perennial forms and have low-growing (they may reach 16 in) or sprawling habits. Glossy, dark green, lanceolate leaves grow from woody stems in summer and white to lilac flowers are grouped in terminal spikes.

CONDITIONS

Climate   Plants do not like very cold, wet winters. As a native of the Mediterranean region, savory grows best in warm climates. Winter savory can withstand much colder temperatures than the summer variety. Neither variety of savory is suited to growing in the tropics.

Aspect   Prefer to be grown in full sun.

Soil   Like well-drained, alkaline soils. If necessary, dress beds with lime, 7 oz per square yard. Summer savory prefers slightly rich soil and makes an ideal herb to grow in containers; winter savory favors a less rich, sandy soil.

GROWING METHOD

Planting   Sow seeds into final garden position in spring, after the weather has warmed up. Lightly cover with soil and keep the soil damp. Thin established seedlings to 18 in apart and support by mounding soil around the base. Winter savory is best propagated by cuttings and root division during spring or autumn. Remove upper and lower leaves of 3–4 in long cuttings and plant trimmed stem in a mixture of two-thirds coarse sand and one-third peat moss. Water container and cover it with plastic supported on a frame. Plant out when new leaves appear and a root structure develops. Pieces of the divided root of parent plant can be potted up and later planted in the open garden.

THE ANCIENT ROMANS considered savory to be the most delightfully fragrant of all herbs: the poet Virgil sang its praises.

WINTER SAVORY is so called because it is available in winter when summer savory dies off—but you can, of course, eat it in summer too.

Watering   Water these plants regularly although both summer and winter savories are able to tolerate dry conditions.

Fertilizing   Summer savory needs to be given side applications of liquid fertilizer every two or three weeks during the spring and summer growth cycle.

Problems   Savories are not worried by pests or diseases to any great extent with the exception of root rot, which sometimes can affect the winter varieties. Good drainage is essential for these plants, or alternatively you can rotate crops every three years.

Pruning   Winter savory can be pruned in autumn after it has finished flowering (as a protection against winter cold) and again in early spring—this will also provide cuttings from which you can grow new plants.

HARVESTING

Picking   Fresh leaves of both summer and winter varieties can be picked at any time for immediate use or for drying.

Storage   Dry leaves in a cool, airy space and then store them in airtight jars.

Freezing   Pack sprigs in plastic wrap and freeze for up to 6 months.

USES

Culinary   Summer savory has a peppery flavor and is called the "bean" herb as it complements beans and other vegetables. It is also used in herb vinegars and butters. Winter savory has a stronger aroma and more piney taste: use it with game meats and terrines. Either type can be used to make savory tea.

SORREL

Rumex scutatus

ELIZABETHAN COOKS used to wrap tough meat in sorrel leaves to tenderize it and add piquant flavor. They also used to make "green sauce" from chopped young leaves, vinegar and sugar. Try it with roast lamb, as a change from mint sauce.

FEATURES

French sorrel is a sprawling perennial herb that grows to 20 in high. Its heart-shaped leaves are carried on erect stems rather resembling a dock weed. Another member of the family, *R. acetosa*, is known commonly as sour dock. Small green flowers appear on long stalks in summer.

CONDITIONS

Climate   Prefers moist, warm climates but grows in cooler regions; tolerates some dryness. Grow as a cool season annual in the tropics.

Aspect   Prefers sun or semi-shade but needs protection from winter frosts.

Soil   Needs light, average soil. To promote strong leaf growth, add animal manures to the soil and mulch well. Tolerates slightly acidic soils.

GROWING METHOD

Planting   Sow seed directly into the garden during spring. Thin seedlings to 12 in apart. Mature plants can be divided in autumn or early spring. To do this, dig up older plants, trim the leaves and stems and replant the divided portions 12–16 in apart.

Watering   Water regularly. If the soil is left to dry out, the leaves wilt and burn off.

Fertilizing   Give an application of high nitrogen liquid or soluble fertilizer monthly.

Problems   Snails and slugs attack leaves. Pick them off by hand or set stale beer traps among the beds. (Fill a saucer with beer and set it into the ground with the rim at soil level.) If leaf miners attack the plant, remove and destroy infested leaves.

Pruning   If you are not growing plants for seed, pinch out the seed-bearing stalks as they appear.

HARVESTING

Picking   Leaves can be picked throughout the growing season as required. Always pick from the outside of the clump.

Storage   Freshly picked leaves will keep in the refrigerator for a few days if they are stored in a plastic bag.

Freezing   Pack leaves in plastic wrap and freeze for up to 6 months.

USES

Culinary   Sorrel used to be cooked and eaten like spinach. Today, because we know it contains a lot of oxalic acid, we use only the small leaves, which have a lemony flavor, in salads or they can be made into a delicious soup.

TANSY
Tanacetum vulgare

FEATURES

Growing over 3 ft tall, tansy is a sprawling perennial with gray-green, finely divided, ferny foliage and heads of yellow, button-like flowers in summer and autumn. The leaves are aromatic and bitter to the taste and the whole plant dies back to ground level over winter. It spreads out by means of creeping roots and can become quite large over time. In smaller areas it will need to be reduced regularly.

CONDITIONS

Climate   Grows in cool and warm areas but is not well suited to the tropics.

Aspect   Full sun, part-shade or bright, dappled shade are equally suitable for tansy, although full sun produces more compact growth and many more flowers.

Soil   Any well-drained soil will do; able to grow almost anywhere its seed falls.

GROWING METHOD

Planting   Dividing the roots of an established plant is the easiest way to start a new plant quickly. Lift the parent in early spring and cut or pull the creeping roots into sections, each with its own roots. Replant immediately into the permanent site. Tansy may also be started from seed sown in spring or early autumn or from cuttings of semi-ripe stems that are taken in late spring and rooted in a moist, sandy potting mix.

Watering   Water sparingly but deeply. In coastal areas, tansy can usually get by on rain.

Fertilizing   No fertilizing is needed.

Problems   No particular problems.

Pruning   Cut the plants to the ground in middle to late autumn (early winter in warm areas). New growth will appear in spring.

HARVESTING

Picking   Pick leafy stems anytime during the warmer months. If flower stems are to be cut, do this when they are freshly opened rather than when they are old.

Storage   Both leaves and flowers can be stored dry. To dry, tie bunches together and hang them in a dim, well-ventilated place or lay out on drying racks. When the leaves are dry, remove them from their stems and store in airtight jars. Take the dried flowers off the stems and store the flowers in airtight jars.

THE AROMA OF TANSY is said to deter flies, and people used to place sprigs of tansy leaves on meat to keep flies off it.

Freezing   Not suitable for freezing.

USES

Cosmetic   Tansy leaves can be used to make a delightful skin freshener.

Medicinal   Although tansy can be taken for medicinal purposes, it must only be administered by a trained herbal practitioner. Tansy has toxic properties and can be easily taken to excess.

Gardening   Tansy is a lovely, silvery green plant with very attractive flowers and an aroma that is very pleasant in the garden. Grow it in borders of mixed flowers or in big containers that prevent its unwanted spread.

TARRAGON
Artemisia dracunculus

FEATURES

The two culinary varieties grown are French tarragon (*A. dracunculus*) and Russian or "false" tarragon (*A. dracunculus* var. *dracunculoides*). French tarragon is a perennial herb that spreads by rhizomes or underground stems, sending up erect stems to a height of 16–20 in or more. Leaves are olive green and have an anise flavor. It dies down over winter and regenerates in spring. It must be propagated by division. The tarragon seed offered by some nurseries is Russian tarragon. This keeps some of its foliage and is more vigorous but has a much more bitter flavor. Tarragon needs to be replanted every few years as plants lose their vigor over time. White or greenish flowers appear in late summer.

CONDITIONS

Climate   Cool and warm climates provide the best conditions but tarragon grows well in hot, arid areas if watered regularly. If winters are not cool enough to cause the plant to go dormant, it will be short lived.

Aspect   Prefers full sun or partial shade.

Soil   Needs well-drained, sandy soils that do not hold moisture for too long, especially over winter when the rhizomes may rot. Dig in some organic matter such as compost and animal manures.

GROWING METHOD

Planting   Propagate by root division. Lift the plant during spring, divide it and replant the pieces in pots or in the garden spaced 24 in apart.

Watering   Keep well watered but ease off over winter. Soils should be damp but not soggy.

Fertilizing   Apply complete plant food once in early spring. Mulch French tarragon over winter when it has died down.

Problems   No specific pests but it does suffer from downy and powdery mildew. Fungal growths may appear on leaves, which wilt and die. Remove affected plants and burn them. Root rot may also be a problem.

Pruning   Pick out the flower stems to promote leaf growth.

PROLONGED HEAT destroys the flavor of fresh tarragon, and so add it at the end of cooking. Dried tarragon is not affected in this way.

HARVESTING

Picking   Pick leaves during summer but take care not to bruise them.

Storage   Leaves can be dried although much of the flavor and some of the color will be lost in the process. Place them on racks or hang stems in bunches in a warm, dry place, and then store them in airtight jars. Leaves can be preserved in vinegar.

Freezing   Wrap leaves in plastic wrap and freeze for up to 6 months.

USES

Culinary   Tarragon is one of the classic French fines herbes used to enhance the flavors of sundry foods from fish, meat and dairy foods to herbed vinegars, butters, creamy sauces, vegetables and soups. Leaves of Russian tarragon lack the aromatic oils of the French variety.

THYME
Thymus

A GARDEN SEAT surrounded by a collection of thymes makes a fragrant resting place. Position the creeping thyme (Thymus serpyllum) *in front of the seat as it can be trodden on. Thyme has several cultivars, with white, pink or magenta flowers in spring.*

FEATURES

Thyme is one of the most common of garden herbs, and many varieties are grown. Most thymes are low, creeping plants although some will grow to 10–12 in. The shape of the bush and the color and aroma of the leaves depends on the variety. Not all thymes are used in cooking, the most commonly used varieties including lemon-scented thyme (*T.* x *citriodorus*), caraway thyme (*T. herba-barona*), common garden thyme (*T. vulgaris*), orange thyme (*T. vulgaris* 'Fragrantissimus') and silver posie thyme (*T. vulgaris* 'Silver Posie'). Thyme plants are perennials but usually need replacing every two or three years.

CONDITIONS

Climate Warm, dry climates are best, although low, creeping varieties grow better in colder areas.

Aspect Prefers full sun or partial shade and a light, well-drained soil.

Soil Does not need very rich soil but adding some compost will help to keep the soil friable. The soil should not be too acid: if necessary, add lime to the garden bed at the rate of 4 oz per square yard.

GROWING METHOD

Planting Sow seeds in spring or autumn in clumps in flat trays containing damp seed-raising mix. Mist spray trays until seeds germinate, usually within a week. When seedlings are 4 in tall, place outside for a week to harden seedlings and then transplant into garden. Dividing mature plants is one method of propagation. During spring or summer, gently lift the parent plant, cut it into two or three sections, each with a good root formation, and then place elsewhere in the garden. Layering is another method of propagation.

Watering	Do not overwater. Thymes prefer a dryish soil. Water adequately in dry spells.
Fertilizing	No fertilizer needed.
Problems	Spider mite, which feeds by sucking juice, can affect this herb. Treat with a recommended insecticidal spray. Root rot will set in if the soil is not well drained and is allowed to become waterlogged.
Pruning	Prune or clip to prevent woodiness.

HARVESTING

Picking	Fresh leaves and flowers can be picked as required or the whole plant can be cut back to within 2 in of the ground in summer and the leaves dried.
Storage	Leaves are dried on the stem by hanging branches in a warm, airy place. Branches are then stripped and stored in airtight jars.
Freezing	Pack in small airtight containers or plastic wrap; can be frozen for up to 6 months.

USES

Culinary	Thyme is a classic component of the French bouquet garni. Varieties of thyme add special, individual flavors to many dishes. Both leaves and flowers can be eaten fresh in salads or used as garnishes or as a flavoring to honey, vinegars, stuffings, butters or teas.
Gardening	Thymes can be grown for their decorative effect as their low, matting habit makes them excellent edging or rockery plants.

'SILVER POSIE,' a small, sprawling shrub with silvery-gray leaves and abundant pale flowers in spring, here offers scent to the passer-by.

ANCIENT GREEKS AND ROMANS considered thyme honey the finest of all, and many modern connoisseurs of honey agree with them.

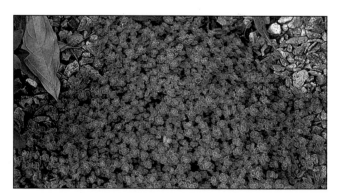

WOOLLY THYME is almost prostrate in habit, its leaves covered in gray fur. The flowers are pale pink but not very abundant.

COMMON THYME, Thymus vulgaris, here sprawls over a carpet of creeping thyme, sometimes called "Shakespeare's thyme."

VIETNAMESE MINT
Polygonum odoratum

FEATURES

Vietnamese mint is a very aromatic, creeping perennial that may grow to nearly 3 ft tall in ideal conditions. The reddish stems are jointed at leaf junctions, and wherever they touch the ground roots will form. The lanceolate leaves are about 3 in long, olive green with a brownish red marking on the upper side. Small, pink flowers are produced at the ends of the stems in spring and summer.

CONDITIONS

Climate   Grows best in a warm or tropical climate as it is not hardy to temperatures that are much below freezing.

Aspect   Plant Vietnamese mint in bright, dappled shade or where it receives shade during the hotter part of the day in summer. It grows in full sun if kept well watered. It is not a plant for hot, dry spots.

Soil   Vietnamese mint needs fertile, well-drained soil that contains enough rotted organic matter to retain the moisture. It enjoys good conditions and can get out of hand very quickly if care is not taken to control excess growth regularly.

GROWING METHOD

Planting   As Vietnamese mint stems root where they touch the ground, new plants are easily created by detaching the newly rooted section from the parent plant and replanting it. Cuttings also root very easily if taken in late spring and summer. The cutting can be taken from the parent plant and then inserted into the ground directly where it is to grow.

Watering   Although Vietnamese mint that has withered from lack of water will recover when rewetted, it grows fastest and best where it has ample water always.

Fertilizing   During spring and summer, water it occasionally with soluble fertilizer that contains a high proportion of nitrogen or sprinkle it with a ration of complete plant food once in spring and again in summer.

Problems   No particular problems apart from the plant's ability to spread fast.

VIETNAMESE MINT is not related to the usual mints but it resembles them in its love of moist places, and its invasiveness.

HARVESTING

Picking   Pick individual leaves or stems as required. Vietnamese mint is best used fresh.

Storage   As this plant grows so fast, there is no need to store it.

Freezing   Not suitable for freezing.

USES

Culinary   A popular herb in Vietnamese and other southeast Asian cuisines, Vietnamese mint is added during cooking and is also a salad ingredient. It has a peppery taste which is pleasant in small amounts.

VIOLET
Viola odorata

FEATURES

Violets are low-growing perennials just 6 in tall with a wider spread. The dark green leaves are roundish or kidney-shaped with scalloped edges. Small, very sweetly fragrant flowers appear on short stalks in winter and early spring. They are usually violet in color but there are also mauve, yellow and white forms. Violets spread rapidly by creeping roots.

CONDITIONS

Climate Grows in cool or warm climates but dislikes the tropics or hot, dry summers.

Aspect Sun in winter and bright dappled shade in summer are ideal. Where summers are mild, violets will tolerate full sun. They do not tolerate hot, dry winds. Flowering is disappointing in too much shade.

Soil Violets need deep soil rich in rotted organic matter, preferably from composted fallen leaves. Soil must drain freely but it must also remain moist between showers or watering.

GROWING METHOD

Planting Violets are easily established by division. Lift immediately after flowering and separate the cylindrical runners. Each division should have its own roots but roots usually form later if they are absent. Plant so that the runners are firmly in contact with the soil but not buried. Scatter seed, collected from ripe but unopened seed pods, where it is to grow or, for better germination, onto trays of seed-raising mix. Cover lightly, keep moist and place trays in a bright but shady and cool place. Transplant seedlings when they are big enough to handle.

Watering Once established, violets can usually get by on rain where it falls regularly, if soil conditions suit them. If they never go dry for long periods, violets will flourish.

Fertilizing Place a mulch of rotted manure around plants, but not over the root crown, each spring (this can be hard in a densely planted area), or sprinkle a ration of complete plant food over the plants in spring. Once or twice during summer, water over with a liquid, organic fertilizer or seaweed-based soil conditioner.

VIOLETS are notoriously shy: if your flowers hide, cut plants back in winter so the flowers are displayed against fresh, not-too-tall growth.

Problems Lay bait for slugs and snails, which chew holes in the leaves and destroy flowers. Spider mites and aphids can also damage plants by sucking sap. You can buy predatory mites to help control the spider mites; aphids are easily controlled with low toxicity pyrethrum, garlic or fatty acid sprays. If plants fail to flower, the cause may be too much or too heavy shade or too much high nitrogen fertilizer.

Pruning No pruning is necessary, but if flowers fail to form cut all the leaves off in early winter to encourage spring bloom.

HARVESTING

Picking Flowers are picked as soon as they open and leaves may be picked as needed.

Storage Flowers may be crystallized for later use.

Freezing Not suitable for freezing.

USES

Culinary Crystallized flowers are used to decorate cakes or eaten as a sweet treat.

Medicinal An infusion of the leaves and flowers can be taken to relieve the symptoms of colds.

Craft Violets are used in potpourris.

Gardening Violets are a very desirable groundcover in partly shaded areas. Posies of cut flowers will fill a room with fragrance.

WATERCRESS

Nasturtium officinale

DESPITE ITS PEPPERINESS, watercress quenches thirst—at least for a little while—and hunters used to carry sprigs for refreshment.

WATERCRESS needs abundant moisture. One way to give it enough is to grow it as market gardeners do, in an easily flooded trench.

FEATURES

Although European in origin, watercress is now widely used in Asian cuisines. It is a low-growing perennial (to 8 in) with a spreading habit. Round, dark green leaves composed of several leaflets have a peppery mustard flavor and are carried on fleshy stems. These either float or are submerged in shallow, moving water or root in rich, wet soil. Clusters of small white flowers appear in early summer.

CONDITIONS

Climate   Warm, moist climates are ideal. In warm climates grow mostly in winter, in cooler zones grow through spring and autumn.

Aspect   Prefers a wet, shady place, such as a pond or stream that is protected from both strong winds and winter frosts. A pot or tub that can be kept damp is also suitable.

Soil   Ideal conditions resemble a clean, running stream. If growing watercress in a container, use very damp, rich soil and top it off occasionally with well-rotted garden compost. Do not let the water stagnate: drain off some once a week and top off up with fresh water each time. The water should be alkaline and around 50°F.

GROWING METHOD

Planting   Grow by root division of a mature plant. Place new pieces into a container with good quality potting mix and then lower it into a waterbed. Seeds can also be sown in spring by placing them on a constantly damp seed-raising mix. Transplant seedlings to a permanent position when they are about 3 in tall.

Watering   Requires a great deal of water.

Fertilizing   Apply high nitrogen, soluble plant food every two weeks from spring to late summer.

Problems   Watercress is sometimes subject to fungal diseases, which cause rotting of stems and death of leaves. Remove infected plants.

HARVESTING

Picking   Pick leaves as required.

Storage   Freshly picked leaves will keep in fresh cold water or sealed plastic bags in the refrigerator for a couple of days.

Freezing   Seal in plastic wrap and freeze for up to 6 months.

USES

Culinary   Watercress is rich in vitamin C and used raw in salads, sandwiches or as a garnish. Chinese tend to cook the herb, making delicious soups.

WORMWOOD
Artemisia

FEATURES

There are many species of wormwood, or artemisa, all with aromatic foliage and pleasant, but not particularly showy, yellow flowers. Sizes and habits, however, vary enormously between species, some being ground huggers, others being medium-sized, upright shrubs. Leaf shape and color varies, too, and combinations of different wormwood plants can make very attractive plantings with a silver and gray theme.

CONDITIONS

Climate   Native to the Mediterranean region, wormwood does best in cool or warm climates where summers are relatively dry but winters are wet. In areas of summer rain and high humidity, grow these plants in very well-drained, sandy soil and in an open, breezy, sunny situation. Plants are very tolerant of summer droughts.

Aspect   Full sun is essential, as is an open position to ensure good air movement around plant.

Soil   Grows best in moderately fertile, very well-drained soil that contains a small proportion of rotted organic matter.

GROWING METHOD

Planting   Wormwood can be started from cuttings taken in late spring and rooted in small pots of moist, sandy potting mix kept in a bright but not fully sunny spot. They may also be grown from seed sown just beneath the surface, either where plants are to grow or in pots or trays of seed-raising mix. Sow seed in autumn just as the winter rain is starting.

Watering   Very little water is needed except in areas where the cooler months are dry. In very hot, semi-arid areas, wormwood may need the odd, deep soaking in summer.

Fertilizing   A mulch of rotted manure or compost laid under and beyond the plant's foliage canopy (but not right up against the trunk) is all the feeding required. Otherwise, sprinkle a handful of bone meal under the outer edge of the foliage canopy in early spring.

Problems   No particular problems except in areas of summer rain and high humidity where plants are subject to root rot and foliage diseases, and are often short lived.

DESPITE ITS BITTERNESS, wormwood used to be thought a potent aphrodisiac—hence its other names of "lad's love" and "maid's ruin."

Pruning   Cut perennial species back to ground level in middle to late autumn or after frosts have started. Shrubby types may be sheared all over in early spring to make them more compact, or cut them back hard in spring if the shrub has become too big and/or untidy.

HARVESTING

Picking   Leaves are harvested by picking whole stems on a hot, dry morning in early summer. Tie stems together and hang them upside down in a dim, airy place to dry.

Storage   Dried leaves may be stored in airtight jars.

Freezing   Not suitable for freezing.

USES

Medicinal   Different parts of different types of wormwood have various medicinal uses but do not take any of these herbs without the supervision of a trained herbalist.

Gardening   All wormwoods have beautiful foliage and a pleasant aroma. A strong infusion of the leaves sprayed onto vegetables or ornamentals repels caterpillars and snails; just having the plants nearby will drive some pests away.

YARROW
Achillea millefolium

FEATURES

Yarrow is a low, mat-forming perennial that has dense, dark green, fern-like foliage. Flat heads of small flowers appear on top of tall, mostly leafless stems during the later summer months and in autumn. They may be white, pink or yellow. This vigorous grower is well suited to growing in rockeries or on banks.

CONDITIONS

Climate Yarrow is best grown in cool climates where winters are always frosty but it grows reasonably well in warmer areas. It is not suitable for the tropics.

Aspect Full sun is essential.

Soil Well-drained, not-too-rich soil is ideal. Plants grow lax, flower poorly and die young in over-rich soil. They will rot if soil stays wet for long periods after rain or watering.

GROWING METHOD

Planting Establish yarrow in new areas by dividing the roots of mature plants in early spring or autumn. It may also be started from seed sown in spring in trays of moist seed-raising mix. Just cover the seed and place the containers in a warm, bright but shaded spot until germination is complete. Gradually expose containers to more and more sun, and then transplant seedlings into their final site when they are big enough.

Watering Water deeply but only occasionally. Yarrow does not require constant moisture as it has deep roots that will find water at lower levels in the soil.

Fertilizing No fertilizing is necessary.

Problems No particular problems.

Pruning Cut plants to the ground in middle to late autumn or after frosts have started. New growth will appear in spring.

HARVESTING

Picking Harvest leafy stems and flowers on a dry morning when plants are in the early stages of full bloom. Tie them together and hang them upside down in a dry, dim, airy place. If they are to be used to make dried arrangements, hang each flower stem separately.

YARROW used to be grown in English churchyards to mock the dead, who supposedly were there because they hadn't eaten their yarrow broth.

Storage When the stems are dry, remove the flowers and leaves from their stems, crumble the leaves and break up all the stems into small pieces. Mix stems, leaves and flowers together and store the mixture in airtight jars.

Freezing Not suitable for freezing.

USES

Culinary Young, small leaves have a slightly bitter flavor. Add a few, chopped young leaves to salads or sandwiches to give them a pleasantly sharp taste.

Medicinal Herbal tea made from the dried stems, leaves and flowers is a good general pick-me-up, blood cleanser, tonic for the kidneys and, reputedly, a slimming aid.

Gardening Yarrow is a good choice for informal or meadow-style plantings, or for planting on dry, infertile banks where other flowers are difficult to grow. It is not at all spectacular in bloom but it does have the slightly unkempt look of a wildflower.

HERBS FOR THE KITCHEN

For thousands of years herbs have been indispensable additions to the cooking pot. Their incomparable fragrances and flavors can also be captured in herb butters, used to enliven vinegars and combined to make fines herbes *and* bouquet garni—*essentials in any well-stocked pantry. Herbs are also reputed to have soothing and healing properties when taken in herb teas.*

A thriving herb garden will allow you to experiment and create your own delicious recipes. Use them fresh or dried (see page 84 for instructions on how to dry herbs), but remember that fresh herbs are often less sharp in flavor then dried ones. Herbs can also vary in strength according to the season, so do taste as you add them to a recipe. And if the garden is overflowing with herbs, why not turn them into gifts for your friends and family: the butters, vinegars, teas and other recipes in this section will get you started.

LEFT: Herbs are not indoor plants but a sunny spot on the verandah just outside the kitchen is ideal—and very convenient. When grown in pretty painted pots like here they even become a decorative feature.

HERBAL TEAS

Herbal teas are growing in popularity. They can be made from one herb or a mixture of several, with flowers or spices added if desired. Some teas are made from herb flowers such as chamomile, others are made from the seeds, roots or bark of anise, dandelion and ginger. Tisanes are teas that have been brewed from the leaves of herbs.

Certain herbs have a stronger flavor than others and so less is needed, but in general about 3 teaspoons of chopped herbs is sufficient for one cup. If the herbs have been dried, they are already concentrated and no more than a level teaspooon is necessary. Herbal teas can be made by infusion, in much the same way as normal tea. Steep 2–3 teaspoons of leaves in very hot water for five minutes, being sure to keep the infusion covered to prevent the escape of steam. (If you use a teapot, keep it just for herbal teas.) Then use a strainer as you pour it into the cup. Teas can also be made by decoction, which involves boiling herb seeds, roots or bark and some leaves in water for 15–20 minutes to draw out the flavors.

Herbal teas may be served hot or cold. If they are served iced, they should be made slightly stronger to allow for dilution as the ice cubes melt. For variety and a wonderful blend of flavors, fresh fruit juice can be added to cold teas. Sugar or honey can be added to teas as a sweetener, but most herbal teas are perfect as they are.

HERBAL TEAS can replace more conventional tea and coffee on any occasion. Drink them in the morning, for lunch or afternoon tea, or after dinner.

ANGELICA TEA

 Infuse 3 teaspoons of fresh chopped leaves in 1 cup of boiling water for a calming drink, perfect before sleeping. This tea should not be taken by diabetics (because of its sugar content) or pregnant women, but it is a useful remedy for indigestion, coughs, colds, flatulence and rheumatism.

BASIL TEA

 Infuse 3 teaspoons of fresh chopped leaves in 1 cup of boiling water. Basil tea is used to reduce travel sickness and morning sickness in pregnant women.

BERGAMOT TEA

 Infuse 3 teaspoons of leaves and flowers in 1 cup of boiling water. Use bergamot tea for sore throats and chest ailments.

CARAWAY TEA

 Pour 1 cup of boiling water over 2 teaspoons of crushed seeds and let it steep for 5 minutes. Strain before drinking. Caraway tea is beneficial for the kidneys, glands and digestion.

CHAMOMILE TEA

Add dried or fresh chamomile flowers to a saucepan of boiling water, cover and simmer for 1 minute. Remove from the heat and let stand for a few minutes; then strain and drink. Do not drink large quantities of this tea, and it should be avoided in pregnancy. Chamomile tea is excellent as a bedtime drink, for relieving tension or menstrual pain.

DANDELION TEA

Infuse 5–6 leaves (remove stems and shred leaves first) in 1 cup of boiling water for a tasty drink that acts as a diuretic and mild laxative. This tea is often useful for relieving the symptoms of rheumatism.

DILL TEA

Pour 1 cup of boiling water over 2 teaspoons of crushed seeds and let it steep for 5 minutes. Strain before drinking. Dill seed tea has many uses, for poor digestion, flatulence, indigestion and stomach upsets, and as a mild tranquillizer and sleep inducer.

FENNEL TEA

Pour 1 cup of boiling water over 2 teaspoons of crushed seeds and let it steep for 5 minutes. Strain before drinking. This is a mild diuretic and laxative, or pads of cotton wool can be soaked in cool tea and dabbed on tired eyes. Avoid consuming large amounts of fennel tea during pregnancy.

LEMON BALM TEA

Infuse 3 teaspoons of fresh leaves in 1 cup of boiling water. Lemon balm tea relieves headaches and toothache, as well as tension, and it can help in the early stages of a cold.

LEMON GRASS TEA

Tie a piece of lemon grass into a knot and infuse it in 1 cup of boiling water. This mild diuretic also helps clear the skin.

LOVAGE TEA

Infuse 3 teaspoons of fresh leaves or 1 teaspoon of dried leaves in 1 cup of boiling water. A very mild diuretic, lovage tea is good for the kidneys and stimulates the appetite.

MINT TEA

Infuse 3 teaspoons of fresh spearmint or peppermint leaves or 1 teaspoon of dried leaves in 1 cup of boiling water. Mint tea clears the head and sweetens the breath, and it is good for digestion. It can be drunk hot, or cold with ice cubes and lemon slices. Spearmint is milder than peppermint but more fragrant.

PARSLEY TEA

Infuse 3 teaspoons of fresh leaves or 1 teaspoon of dried leaves in 1 cup of boiling water. Drunk hot, parsley tea is a diuretic and it will help those suffering from anaemia.

ROSEMARY TEA

Infuse 3 teaspoons of fresh leaves in 1 cup of boiling water. This tea is used for headaches, to improve the memory and as a bedtime drink.

SAGE TEA

Infuse 3 teaspoons of fresh leaves in 1 cup of boiling water. Sage tea is used for constipation and rheumatism and is good for the liver and general health. Epileptics and pregnant women should avoid this tea.

SAVORY TEA

Infuse 3 teaspoons of fresh leaves or 1 teaspoon of dried leaves in 1 cup of boiling water. Either summer or winter savory can be used as a general tonic.

THYME TEA

Infuse 3 teaspoons of fresh leaves or 1 teaspoon of dried leaves in 1 cup of boiling water. Thyme tea is used for tension headaches, overtiredness, sore throats, colds or exposure to smokey atmospheres. It should be avoided during pregnancy. Cooled thyme tea can be used as a mouthwash.

CONDIMENTS

FRESH FROM THE GARDEN, herbs are a delightful addition to a variety of foods and condiments. Pick them as you need them.

HERB VINEGARS

Freshly picked herbs are a wonderful addition to a good white wine vinegar or cider vinegar. Herb vinegars add flavor and variety to salad dressings, marinades and sauces.

Pick the herbs, wash them and pat them dry. Loosely fill a clean jar with them, pour on enough vinegar to fill the jar and cap. Store in a warm place for about three weeks or until the vinegar is fully flavored. If a stronger taste is required, strain and add fresh herbs. When the vinegar is ready, strain it and pour it into attractive bottles. Label the bottles, and add a fresh sprig of the herb to the bottle for decoration and identification.

Use basil, chives, dill, fennel, garlic, lovage, marjoram, mint, oregano, rosemary, sage, savory, tarragon or thyme for vinegars.

HERB BUTTERS

Many herbs don't freeze particularly well, and one of the best ways of preserving their flavor for future use is to make a herb butter, which can be frozen for up to three months. The butters can then be used on breadsticks, pasta, vegetables, fish, grilled or barbecued meats.

Suitable herbs for making butters are basil, chervil, chives, dill, garlic, lovage, oregano, parsley, rosemary, sage, tarragon and thyme. Herbs can also be used in combination, for example basil, chives and oregano, or dill, chives and parsley.

For every 8 oz of softened butter, mix in three tablespoons of freshly chopped herbs and the juice of one lemon. Pound the butter until smooth and roll into logs. Wrap in plastic wrap or foil, and freeze. Or they can be frozen in ice cube trays to make smaller portions.

FRESH BOUQUET GARNI

A bouquet garni is a small bunch of fresh herbs used to flavor stocks, soups, stews and sauces. To make one, tie together two sprigs of parsley, a sprig of thyme and a bay leaf. A sprig of marjoram, rosemary or sage and a piece of celery is sometimes included. Remove and discard the bouquet garni once the dish is cooked. If you prefer, chop the herbs and place them on a small square (about 6 in square) of muslin. Gather the corners together and tie with a long string that can be left dangling over the edge of the pot for easy removal.

Bouquet garni can also be made from herbs that have been dried for a few days first.

FINES HERBES

This useful seasoning is a fine addition to any kitchen and a jar of *fines herbes* makes a good gift. Use them in small quantities in vegetable, egg, chicken and fish dishes, or in soups, salads and sauces. Add them at the end of cooking to retain their fresh flavor.

Finely chop equal quantities of chervil, chives, tarragon and, if desired, parsley.

CRYSTALLIZED FLOWERS

Newly opened borage or violet flowers can be crystallized and used to decorate cakes and desserts. Take off the stems and handle the flowers as little as possible. Place them on greaseproof paper and brush the petals lightly with egg white. Use a small paintbrush and be sure to coat them well. Dust them with superfine sugar and leave them to dry at room temperature. Store in an airtight container.

USING HERBS IN COOKING

ASIAN DISHES

fresh basil leaves;
fresh coriander leaves,
stems and roots;
garlic chives;
garlic; ginger;
fresh lemon grass;
fresh Vietnamese mint

BEANS

bay leaves; coriander
seeds; garlic; mint;
parsley; savory

BEEF

basil; bay leaves;
coriander leaves and
seeds; garlic; ginger;
horseradish; mint;
oregano; parsley;
thyme

BISCUITS

anise; dill or fennel seeds

BREAD

anise; dill or fennel seeds

CABBAGE

anise; dried basil;
dill and fennel seeds

CAKES

anise; dill or fennel
seeds; candied angelica
stems and crystallised
violet or borage flowers
for decorating

CHEESE

basil; fresh chervil;
chives; fresh dill; garlic;
oregano; fresh parsley;
fresh rocket; thyme

CHICKEN

basil; fresh chervil;
chives; fresh coriander
leaves, stems and roots;
coriander seeds;
garlic; ginger;
fresh lemon balm;
fresh lemon grass;
marjoram; oregano;
parsley; rosemary; sage;
savory; tarragon; thyme

EGGS

basil; fresh chervil;
chives; dill; marjoram;
oregano; parsley; savory;
tarragon; thyme

FISH

basil; chervil; chives;
coriander leaves and
seeds; dill; fennel leaves,
seeds and bulb; garlic;
ginger; horseradish;
fresh lemon balm;
fresh lemon grass;
marjoram; oregano;
parsley; fresh rocket;
tarragon; thyme

FRENCH DISHES

bay leaves; chervil;
chives; garlic; parsley;
rosemary; sage;
tarragon; thyme

FRUIT

fresh bergamot leaves
and flowers;
fresh young borage leaves
and flowers;
fresh lemon balm leaves;
fresh lemon verbena
leaves

GAME

bay leaves; fresh parsley;
rosemary

INDIAN DISHES

coriander seeds;
curry leaves;
fennel seeds; garlic;
fresh grated ginger

ITALIAN DISHES

anise seed; basil;
chicory; fennel leaves,
seeds and bulb; garlic;
marjoram; oregano;
parsley; fresh rocket;
rosemary; sage;
savory; thyme

LAMB

basil; bay leaves;
coriander leaves and
seeds; dill; garlic;
ginger; lemon balm;
marjoram; mint;
parsley; rosemary;
thyme

MEXICAN DISHES

coriander leaves and
seeds; oregano; parsley

PICKLES

anise; coriander;
dill and fennel seeds;
ginger; garlic

PORK

anise leaves and seeds;
coriander leaves and
seeds; dill leaves and
seeds; garlic; ginger;
marjoram; oregano;
sage; thyme

POTATOES

chives; dill leaves; garlic;
parsley; rosemary; thyme

SALAD DRESSINGS

basil; chives; coriander;
dill; garlic; ginger;
horseradish; lemon grass;
mint; parsley; rosemary;
tarragon; thyme

SALADS

(all fresh) basil;
bergamot leaves and
flowers; young borage
leaves and flowers;
chervil; young chicory
leaves; coriander;
young dandelion leaves;
finely sliced fennel bulb;
nasturtium leaves and
flowers; parsley; rocket;
salad burnet; watercress

SAUCES

basil; bay leaves; chives;
dill; garlic; ginger; mint;
parsley; sage; tarragon

SHELLFISH

basil; chervil; chives;
coriander; dill;
lemon grass; parsley;
tarragon; thyme

TOMATOES

basil; chives; garlic;
marjoram; oregano;
parsley; rocket; thyme

VEAL

basil; garlic; marjoram;
oregano; parsley; sage;
rosemary; tarragon;
thyme

Note: Leaves used can be either fresh or dried unless specified; seeds can be used whole or ground unless specified.

HERB CRAFTS

*Lavender, rosemary, thyme, oregano,
sage and marjoram are among
the most popular herbs for use in craft
and cosmetics. They can be used alone
to yield a fresh, clean aroma, or
combined with flowers such as roses
and scented-leaved geraniums for
a sweeter, gentler fragrance.*

Used fresh or dried, herbs are remarkably versatile. In medieval Europe they were strewn on the floor to counteract unwelcome odors, and they can still be used to perfume the house. Make them into wonderful wreaths or wall hangings, potpourris or sachets. Herbs can be used to perfume the bath, to scent pillows or make skin fresheners, hair rinses or other cosmetics. In fact, they can be readily substituted for flowers in almost any craft idea.

LEFT: Herbs will add a delightful fragrance to many craft items: there's plenty to choose from, ranging from scents that are cool and refreshing to those that are sweet and pervasive.

ABOVE: A pot of sage.

DRYING HERBS

Fresh herbs are more attractive than dried ones and are almost always used in preference to the dried variety. However, you may want to cut and dry herbs that are annuals before they die down, or preserve the cut-away stems of shrubby herbs pruned at the end of summer. Some of the best herbs for drying are bay, thyme, rosemary, marjoram, oregano and sage.

Harvest the herbs on a dry day and divide them into small bunches. Strip a few leaves away from the base of the stem so that they can be tied in neat bunches without mold forming on the stems. Tie the stems firmly and hang the bunches in a warm, airy place away from direct sunlight. Leaves and flowers can also be dried spread on wire frames, newspaper or in shallow baskets. Place the containers in a dry, airy place away from light and gently toss the material each day to help the drying process. When they are completely dry, carefully strip the leaves from the branches and store them in labeled, airtight jars.

HERB POTPOURRIS

Wonderful, fragrant potpourris can be made from herbs, usually combined with rose petals or scented geranium leaves. They are perfect fillings for sachets or pillows, or can be placed in bowls or boxes to perfume the house.

Dry the herbs and flowers as described in the box opposite. Fixatives, such as oakmoss and dried orris root, and essential oils can be purchased from health food shops, some Asian supermarkets and some craft shops.

FLORAL AND HERB POTPOURRI

1 cup rose petals
¼ cup violets
½ cup marigold flowers
½ cup lavender
¼ cup cornflowers
½ cup sweet mixed herbs
1 tablespoon orris root powder
2 teaspoons cinnamon powder
5 drops rose oil
3 drops lavender oil
2 drops lemon oil

Place the dried flowers and herbs in a bowl and gently mix them together with a wooden spoon, being careful not to break the flower petals. Place the orris root and cinnamon in another bowl and, using an eyedropper, add the essential oils. Mix together thoroughly.

Add the orris root and cinnamon mixture to the dried materials and stir with a wooden spoon. Place in a brown paper bag, fold over the top and fasten with a clothes peg. Store in a cool, dark place for two to four weeks and shake the bag gently every few days to blend ingredients. It should then be ready for use.

LEMON SCENTED POTPOURRI

4 cups lemon verbena leaves
1 cup lemon-scented geranium leaves
½ cup basil
½ cup lemon thyme
½ cup dried lemon peel (freshly ground)
½ cup dried orange peel (freshly ground)
½ cup caraway seed
1 cup oakmoss
2 drops lemon verbena oil
2 drops bergamot oil

Mix the leaves together. Mix the peel with the caraway seed. Tear oakmoss into small pieces, place in a bowl and add essential oils. Rub the oil through the oakmoss and mix thoroughly with the leaves, peel and seeds. Place in an airtight container for about a month, stirring occasionally. It will then be ready for use.

LAVENDER AND HERB POTPOURRI

5 cups lavender flowers
1 cup lavender foliage
1 cup mint
1 cup rosemary
1 cup oakmoss
½ cup juniper berries, crushed
½ cup coriander seeds, crushed
2 drops lavender oil

Mix lavender flowers and leaves, and herbs in a bowl. In a separate bowl mix oakmoss, juniper berries and coriander, then add lavender oil and blend it through with your hands. Add this to the dried mixture and mix thoroughly. Store in an airtight container for about a month to allow the scents to mature, stirring occasionally. It will then be ready for use.

LAVENDER MIXTURE

2 cups lavender flowers
2 tablespoons orris root powder
4 drops lavender oil

Mix the flowers and orris root together and then add the oil and mix through. Store in an airtight container for three weeks, shaking occasionally, before using it.

ABOVE: This blue and white bowl is the perfect container for rose-based potpourri.

OPPOSITE PAGE: Potpourri ingredients, including bay leaves, rosemary, rose petals, lavender and orange peel.

FRAGRANT SACHETS

Small bags filled with potpourri mixtures make a fragrant addition to any home. Use them to perfume cupboards, drawers, storage areas or bags, or tie them on doorknobs or chair backs for a decorative effect.

MAKING A SACHET

A sachet is simply a fabric bag, made from a rectangle of fabric folded in half and stitched up two sides. The open side can then be hemmed or trimmed with lace, before the fragrant mixture is added and the bag tied off with a ribbon. Sachets can also be made from a handkerchief or other square of fabric. Just put a spoonful of the mixture in the center of the handkerchief, gather up the corners and tie them together with a pretty ribbon.

Moth sachet
A sachet filled with this mixture will repel moths for up to a year. Make several and tuck them among your woollen clothes and stored blankets.

1 cup rosemary
1 cup tansy
1 cup thyme
1 cup mint
1 cup southernwood
½ cup cloves (freshly ground)
½ cup dried lemon peel (freshly ground)

Crumble all the herbs together and mix with the cloves and lemon peel. Spoon the mixture into sachets and tie with a ribbon.

HERB PILLOW

Some herbs are thought to promote peaceful sleep and sweet dreams, and so a pillow filled with sleep-inducing herbs can be a practical addition to the home. Make this elegant little pillow to put inside a pillowcase or beside the bed, or the mixture can be put into a sachet that is tucked into the pillowcase with your usual pillow.

Make the pillow from two pieces of fabric 12 x 8 in. Place the pieces together with right sides facing and stitch around three sides. If you want to add braid to the pillow, stitch it around the edges of one of the fabric pieces before sewing them together. Turn under the open edges about ¼ in and stitch press studs along the turned under edges to close the pillow. Fill the pillow with the herb mixture and close it.

If you want the pillow to be reusable, make a muslin insert for the fabric pillow. Make it in the same way as the pillow but slightly smaller all around. Put the mixture into the insert and stitch it closed; then slip it inside the pillow. The insert can then be discarded and replaced with a fresh one whenever necessary.

Herb mixture
1 cup dried rosemary
1 cup dried lavender
1 cup dried lemon verbena
1 cup dried lemon thyme
3 cups dried scented geranium leaves

Mix the materials together in a large bowl. If desired, a preservative such as orris root and a drop or two of essential oil can be added (follow the recipes for potpourri on page 85).

BATH BAGS

Bath bags are sachets made from muslin and tied with raffia or string. Tie one to the bath taps and let the water run over the bag—the water will be scented and you will feel relaxed and calm.

The bath bag is used only once, so make the bag small (about 2 x 4 in is a good size) and make half a dozen or so at a time.

Oatmeal mixture
1 cup oatmeal
*1 cup mixed herbs (rosemary, lemon verbena,
    sage or bay leaf)*

Mix the ingredients together in a bowl. Spoon the mixture into the muslin bags and tie them closed. This oatmeal mixture will soften the skin.

Herb mixture
Bath bags can also be made using 2 tablespoons of bran and 1 tablespoon of a herb (lavender, chamomile or rosemary are good choices).

OPPOSITE PAGE. TOP: Sachets filled with herbal mixtures are a delightful way to scent underwear or linen. Make them from coarse-weave cottons, as here, or laces, brocades or muslins—anything that will allow the perfume through.

BOTTOM LEFT: Muslin bath bags can be filled with any herbal mixture to give a wonderfully indulgent bath.

BOTTOM RIGHT: This pillow is a beautiful addition to the bedroom, and when filled with sleep-inducing herbs it's useful, too.

87

HERB WREATH AND POSY

Herbs are well suited to wreaths and other arrangements, whether used fresh or dried, alone or mixed with flowers and foliage. Angelica, bay leaves, bergamot, fennel, lavender, lemon balm, rosemary, sorrel, thyme and wormwood are all useful. The arrangements shown here were made with fresh flowers to be used the same day, but similar ones can be made with dried herbs for a less colorful but longer lasting result.

HERB WREATH

This fresh herb wreath should be made on the day it is needed but it makes a lovely and unusual decoration for a dining area or for the front door. Herbs have been chosen to show a variety of color—several different shades of green leaves and purple basil as well as the light blue flowers of rosemary, the purple ones of the basil and the bright orange of the nasturtiums—and texture, with curly parsley, soft dill and spiky thyme and rosemary.

Dill
Purple basil in flower
Rosemary in flower
Thyme
Parsley, curly and flat-leaved
Mint
Oregano
Nasturtium leaves and flowers
Foam base, 12 in diameter
Green plastic
Stapler
Florists wire
Scissors

Cover the foam base with the green plastic and staple it in position—this will make it less obvious if any glimpses of the base are seen. Tie together small bunches (two or three sprigs) of each of the herbs, and wire each bunch together at the base of the stems, leaving 2 in lengths of wire at the ends. Push the wire ends into the foam base, starting at the top, slanting the bunches and working always in the same direction to give an impression of movement. Cover the top of the base and the top of the sides.

Space the different herbs around the circle to give a good mix of colors and textures. Tuck the last bunches under the first ones.

HERB POSY

This attractive and fragrant little posy would make a delightful table center for a weeekend lunch or outdoor meal, or it could be substituted for a posy of flowers. It is a worthy descendant of the old-fashioned tussie mussie, which was carried to ward off unpleasant smells. Although best when it is first made, this posy should last for several days.

Lavender in flower
Purple basil in flower
Thyme
Chives
Parsley, curly
Variegated rose geranium leaves
Rubber band or string
Length of raffia (optional)

Cut all the herbs with as long stems as is possible. Arrange the sprigs of lavender, basil, thyme and small bunches of the chives together, and then add the parsley and geranium leaves around the outside. Secure the stems with a rubber band and trim the stems to an even length. If desired, tie a length of raffia around the stems as a finishing touch.

ABOVE: This delightful herb posy makes an ideal table decoration for kitchen or dining room.

LEFT: Add color and fragrance with this fresh herb wreath. It can be hung on a door to provide a special welcome, or on a wall to give an instant lift to any room.

Herbal Cosmetics

There are many simple herbal preparations that you can use to tone, clean, moisturize or simply refresh your skin. Hair rinses, too, can be quickly made from herbs.

CHAMOMILE FACE MASK

A very simple face mask can be made from chamomile flowers, honey and bran. It softens the skin and leaves it feeling beautifully smooth and refreshed.

Make an infusion (see page 78), using 1 tablespoon of dried chamomile flowers or 3 tablespoons of fresh ones and 1 cup of boiling water. Allow the infusion to stand for about half an hour and then strain.

Warm 1 teaspoon of honey in a pan and mix it with about 1/3 cup of the chamomile water and 2 tablespoons of bran. Spread it on your face, leave it for about 10 minutes and then wash it off.

FENNEL FACE CLEANSER

This fresh mixture made from fennel seed, buttermilk and honey is a lovely way to cleanse your face naturally.

Crush or roughly chop 1 tablespoon of fennel seed and then pour 1 cup of boiling water over it. Let it stand for about half an hour and then strain it into a small bowl.

Add 2 tablespoons of buttermilk and 1 teaspoon of honey to the fennel seed water and mix it all together.

Pour the resulting mixture into a completely clean container and refrigerate it until it is cool. The cleanser can be taken from the fridge as needed.

FEVERFEW MOISTURIZER

This complexion milk serves as a moisturizer and will help to discourage blackheads and fade skin blemishes.

Place half a cup of fresh feverfew leaves and 1 cup of milk in a saucepan. Simmer for about 20 minutes and leave it to stand. Strain the liquid into a clean container and refrigerate.

Apply it to the skin with cotton balls and let it dry. Rinse off with lukewarm water.

TANSY-LEAF SKIN FRESHENER

This easy-to-make skin freshener has a strong tansy fragrance. Splash it onto your skin straight from the fridge.

Place 1 cup of fresh tansy leaves, 1 cup of water and 1 cup of milk in a small saucepan and bring to the boil. Simmer it for 15 minutes and then leave it to cool. Strain the liquid from the saucepan into a clean container and then refrigerate it.

HAIR RINSES

There are a number of herbs that make useful and fragrant hair rinses, to use after shampooing. Chamomile rinses will brighten fair hair, rosemary rinses will help control greasy hair and add shine to any hair, and sage rinses will darken gray hair.

Make the hair rinse by placing 5 cups of water and 1 cup of chamomile flowers, fresh rosemary tips or sage leaves in a saucepan and bring the mixture to the boil. Simmer it for 15 minutes and let it cool. The sage rinse should stand for several hours. Then strain and bottle it, ready for use.

Always use an old towel to dry your hair after using a herb rinse—sage, in particular, will stain the towel.

HERBAL COSMETICS are simple to make and much cheaper than purchased ones. Packaged in attractive bottles and provided with corks and colorful ribbons, they also make very desirable gifts.

HARVESTING CHART

PLANT COMMON NAME	SUITABLE CLIMATE	SPRING			SUMMER			AUTUMN			WINTER		
		EARLY	MID	LATE	EARLY	MID	LATE	EARLY	MID	LATE	EARLY	MID	LATE
Aloe vera	○◑	○◑	○◑	○◑	○◑	○◑	○◑	○◑	○◑	○	○	○	○
Angelica	●●	●	●	●	●●	●●	●	●					
Anise	○○●	○	○	○	●●	●●	●●	●●	●●			○	○
Apothecary's rose	●●		●	●	●	●		●●	●●				
Basil	○○●	○	○●	○●	●●	●●	●●	●●	○○●	●●	○	○	○
Bay tree	●●	●●	●●	●●	●●	●●	●●	●●	●●	●●	●●	●●	●●
Bergamot	●●		●	●	●●	●●	●●	●	●				
Betony	●●				●●	●●	●●						
Borage	○○●	○●	○○●	○○●	○	●●	●●	●●	○○●	○○●	○●	○●	○●
Caraway	○○●●	○●	○○●	○●	●●●	●●●			○	○	○	○	○
Catmint	○●●		●●	●●	●●	○●●	○●●	○●●	●●	○			
Celery	○●●		○●●	○●●	○●●	○●●	○●●	●●	●●				
Chamomile	●●		●●	●●	●●	●●							
Chervil	○●●	○●	○●●	○●●	○●●	●●	●●	●●	○●●	○	○	○	○
Chicory	○○●●	○●	○○●	○●	●●●	●●●	●●●	○○●●	○○●●	○	○	○●	○●
Chives	○○●●	○	○○●	○●●	●●●	●●●	●●●	●●●	○●●	●●	●●	●●	○
Comfrey	○●●		●●	●●	●●●	●●●	●●●	●●	●●	●●			
Coriander	○○●	○	○●●	○●●	○●●	●●	●●	●●	○●●	○●●	○●●	○●●	○
Curry tree	○●	○●	○●	○●	○●	○●	○●	○●	○●	○●	○●	○●	○●
Dandelion	○●●	●●	●●	●●	●●	●●	●		●●	●●	●●	●●	●●
Dill	○●●	●	●●	●●	●●	●●●	●●●	●●	●●	●●	●	●	●
Elder	○●●				●●	●	●	●●	●●	●			
Evening primrose	○●●	●	●●	●●	○●●	○●●	○●●	●●	●●	●	●	●	●
Fennel	●●		●●	●●	●●	●●	●●						
Feverfew	○●●	○●	○●	○●	○●●	○●●	●	●	●		○		
Galangal	○●							○●	○●				
Garlic	○●●				●	●	●●	○●●	○●●				
Ginger	○●							○●	○●				
Herb Robert	○●●	●●	●●	●●	○●●	●●	●●	●●	●		●	●	●
Horehound	○●●	●●	●●	●●	●●●	●●	●●	●●	●●		●	●	●

CLIMATE KEY   ○ TROPICAL   ◔ WARM   ◑ COOL   ● COLD

Plant Common Name	Suitable Climate	Spring Early	Spring Mid	Spring Late	Summer Early	Summer Mid	Summer Late	Autumn Early	Autumn Mid	Autumn Late	Winter Early	Winter Mid	Winter Late
Horseradish	◔◑				◔◑	◔◑	◔◑	◔◑	◔◑				
Hyssop	◔◑●	◔◑	◔◑	◔◑	◔◑	◔◑●	◔◑●	◔◑	◔◑				
Lavender	◔◑	◔◑	◔◑	◔◑	◔◑	◔◑						◔	◔
Lavender cotton	◔◑	◔◑	◔◑	◔◑	◔◑		◔◑	◔◑	◔◑	◔◑	◔◑	◔◑	◔◑
Lemon balm	○◔◑	○	○◔◑	○◔◑	○◔◑	○◔◑	◔◑				○	○	○
Lemon grass	○◔◑	◔◑	◔◑		○◔◑	○◔◑	○◔◑	○◔◑	○◔◑	◔◑	◔◑	◔◑	◔◑
Lemon verbena	○◔◑	○◔◑	○◔◑	○◔◑	○◔◑	○◔◑	◔◑	○◔◑	○◔◑	◔◑	◔◑	◔◑	◔◑
Lovage	◔◑	○	◔◑	◔◑	◔◑	◔◑	◔◑	◔◑	◔◑	◔◑			
Marjoram	○◔◑	○◔◑	○◔◑	◔◑	◔◑	◔◑	◔◑	○◔◑	○◔◑	○◔◑	◔◑	◔◑	◔◑
Mint	○◔◑●	○◔◑	○◔◑	○◔◑	○◔◑	○◔◑	○◔◑●	○◔◑●	○◔◑	○◔◑	◔◑	◔◑	◔◑
Nasturtium	○◔◑	◔◑	○◔◑	○◔◑	○◔◑	○◔◑	○◔◑	○◔◑	○◔◑	○◔◑	◔◑	◔◑	◔◑
Oregano	○◔◑●	○◔◑	○◔◑	◔◑	◔◑	○◔◑	◔◑●	○◔◑	○◔◑	○◔◑	◔◑	◔◑	◔◑
Orris root	◔◑				◔◑	◔◑							
Parsley	○◔◑●	○◔◑	○◔◑	○◔◑	○◔◑	○◔◑●	○◔◑●	○◔◑	○◔◑	○◔◑	◔◑	◔◑	◔◑
Purslane	○◔◑●	○	○◔◑	○◔◑	○◔◑	○◔◑●	○◔◑●	○◔◑●	○◔◑	◔◑	○	○	○
Rocket	○◔◑	○	○◔◑	◔◑	◔◑	◔◑	◔◑	◔◑	○◔◑	○◔◑	◔◑	◔◑	○
Rosemary	◔◑	◔◑	◔◑	◔	◔◑	◔◑	◔◑	◔◑	◔◑	◔◑	◔◑	◔◑	◔◑
Rue	◔◑	◔◑	◔◑	◔◑	◔◑	◔◑	◔◑	◔◑	◔◑	◔	◔	◔	
Sage	◔◑●	○	◔◑	◔◑	◔◑●	◔◑●	◔◑●	◔◑	◔◑	◔◑	◔	◔	◔
Salad burnet	◔◑●	◔◑	◔◑	◔◑	◔◑	◔◑●	◔◑●	●					
Savory	◔◑	◔◑	◔◑	◔◑	◔◑	◔◑	◔◑	◔◑	◔◑	◔◑	◔◑	◔◑	◔◑
Sorrel	○◔◑●	○◔◑	◔◑	○◔◑●	○◔◑	◔◑	◔◑	○◔◑●	○◔◑	○◔◑	◔◑	◔◑	○
Tansy	◔◑●		◔◑	◔◑	◔◑●	◔◑●	◔◑●	◔◑	◔◑	◔			
Tarragon	◔◑				◔◑	◔◑	◔◑	◔◑	◔◑				
Thyme	◔◑●	◔◑	◔◑	◔◑●	◔◑●	◔◑●	◔◑●	◔◑	◔◑	◔◑	◔◑	◔◑	◔◑
Vietnamese mint	○◔	○◔	○◔	○◔	○◔	○◔	○◔	○◔	○◔	○◔	○	○	○
Violet	◔◑	◔◑	◔◑	◔◑	◔◑	◔◑	◔◑	◔◑	◔◑	◔		◔	◔
Watercress	○◔◑	◔◑	○◔◑	○◔◑	○◔◑	○◔◑	○◔◑	○◔◑	○◔◑	○◔◑	◔◑	◔◑	○
Wormwood	◔◑●				◔◑	◔◑●	●	●					
Yarrow	◔◑●		◔	○	◔◑	◔◑●	●	●					

INDEX

This 1997 Crescent edition is published by Random House Value Publishing, Inc.,
201 East 50th Street, New York, N.Y. 10022
http://www.randomhouse.com/

Random House
New York • Toronto • London • Sydney • Auckland

Originally published by Murdoch Books®, a division of Murdoch Magazines Pty Ltd,
213 Miller Street, North Sydney NSW 2060 Australia

Managing Editor, Craft and Gardening: Christine Eslick
Designer: Jackie Richards
Additional text: Roger Mann
Photographs: Lorna Rose (all unless specified otherwise); Geoffrey Burnie (pp. 16, 18); Denise Greig (pp. 24L, 24R, 51);
Stirling Macoboy (pp. 39, 41, 60, 62 lower R); Andre Martin (pp. 76–77, 79–91); Luis Martin (p. 78); Reg Morrison (p. 10);
Murdoch Books® Picture Library (pp. 29, 32, 50R, 59 top L); Tony Rodd (pp. 35, 64R). Identification photos by Reg
Morrison, Luis Martin, Geoffrey Burnie and Lorna Rose
Stylist: Anne-Maree Unwin (pp. 76–77, 79–91); Mary Harris (p. 78)
Illustrator: Matthew Ottley
CEO & Publisher: Anne Wilson
International Sales Manager: Mark Newman

© Text, design, commissioned photography and illustrations Murdoch Books® 1996

Printed and bound in the United States of America

A CIP catalog record for this book is available from the Library of Congress
ISBN 0-517-18406-0
87654321

Front cover: Purple sage grows among vegetables
Back cover: Top left: rocket; top center: sage; top right: garlic. Bottom left: comfrey; bottom center: horseradish;
bottom right: dandelion
Inside back cover: The variegated nasturtium 'Alaska' and lavender grow beneath a golden-leaved
Robinia pseudo-acacia 'Frisia'
Title page: Lavender